INTERVIEWS
AND
APPRAISALS

Also in the Career PowerTools Series

INTERVIEWS AND APPRAISALS

KAREN HOLMES

ORION BUSINESS
BOOKS

The right of Karen Holmes to be identified as the
author of this work has been asserted by her in
accordance with the Copyright, Designs and
Patents Act 1988.

First published in Great Britain in 1999 by
Orion Business
An imprint of
The Orion Publishing Group Ltd
Orion House
5 Upper St Martin's Lane
London WC2H 9EA

A CIP catalogue record for this book
is available from the British Library.

ISBN 0–75282–100–8

Typeset by Deltatype Ltd, Birkenhead
Printed and bound in Great Britain by
Clays Ltd, St Ives plc

CONTENTS

INTRODUCTION

Once upon a time, getting a job was straightforward. Somebody told you about an employer who needed staff, you went to see them and they told you when you could start. That was 'the interview'. You could then look forward to a lifetime spent working with the same company until you retired clutching a gold watch and a modest pension.

Times have changed. The job for life culture is a thing of the past. If you work in a rapidly changing industry, you may move from job to job every few years in the search for better prospects and greater challenges. Every time you change your job, you will attend an interview. Even if you stay in the same job for many years, you will attend appraisal interviews to assess your performance and discuss your progress. If you are freelance and compete for short contracts, giving presentations (which are little more than elaborate interviews) will be part of your regular routine.

So, interviews are something we can all expect to experience at regular intervals during our working life. How do we cope?

'I associate interviews with major events in my life like getting into university and looking for a job. Each time, such a lot depended on me doing well that I was incredibly nervous. Now the very word "interview" makes me feel a bit sick.'

'I've interviewed hundreds of people – it's part of my job to recruit and select new staff. To me it's nothing special. I suppose I sometimes forget how disturbing the process

can be for the person being interviewed.'

'It's easy to be blasé about interviews if there's nothing much at stake. I get on perfectly well with my manager but during the half hour appraisal interview we have every twelve months, I'm terrified of her.'

'I quite enjoy interviews. I'm given a limited time to sell myself, to argue my case and that's a real challenge. If I get what I want, whether it is a job or a pay rise, I feel like I've won.'

The person who tells you that interviews are 'a piece of cake' is either blessed with tremendous self-confidence or a liar. Whether an interview is for a job, a promotion or a discussion about our career, we know that it is an important event. That makes us nervous, and when we are nervous we may not perform to the best of our ability.

For many people, an interview is a test where they feel they are being judged: Am I good enough to get this job? Have I performed well during the last six months? What do they expect me to achieve next? The 'test' aspect makes them nervous and consequently an interview for any purpose becomes an ordeal. They forget that the essence of an interview is to give both interviewer and interviewee a fair chance to get the information they need.

Interviews should be a two-way process where information is collected by both parties. In a good interview there are no superiors and subordinates, no person holding all the cards. Instead, there is effective dialogue that gives the participants an opportunity to explore issues relevant to the subject they are discussing.

If you accept that viewpoint and see the interview as a constructive experience rather than a judgement, then you have already taken a massive step towards improving your interview technique. Reading this book will help you improve still further.

Interviews and Appraisals makes no outrageous claims. Reading this book will not guarantee that you get the job / the promotion / the pay rise. What it will do is help you understand some of the processes that take place during an interview so you are better equipped to deal with the process. It focuses on the skills you can use to help control the interview and thus present yourself more positively.

Interviews and Appraisals is divided into three parts:

Part one explores selection interviews. In particular, it considers:

- interviews as part of the selection process
- different types of selection interview (one-to-one, panel interviews and sequential interviews)
- the sequence of events in a selection interview (meet and greet, in-depth questioning, closing the interview, etc.)
- tests, their purpose and format
- assessment centres.

Part two looks at how the interview may be used to monitor career progress. By understanding what performance and development review interviews can achieve, you can gain more control over the appraisal process and contribute actively to the management of your own career. In particular, it addresses the following issues:

- different types of appraisal systems, such as performance reviews and development reviews
- the stages of the appraisal process
- who carries out the appraisal? An evaluation of different types of appraisal including appraisal from above, self-appraisal, peer review and 360 degree feedback
- interview styles that you may encounter during appraisal.

Part three develops the skills that will help you perform well at interview, regardless of whether it is for selection or appraisal. You will find out more about:

- preparing for a selection interview – researching the job and the organisation, frequently asked questions, etc.
- preparing for an appraisal interview by defining your own aims and objectives
- presenting a positive image
- nonverbal communication
- verbal communication
- listening skills
- questioning techniques
- negotiating skills
- receiving feedback
- reviewing your performance in a selection interview
- monitoring your progress after an appraisal interview.

As you read, you will come across the Golden Rules. These are simple pointers towards good practice, compiled through research with both interviewers and interviewees. Follow the rules and you won't go far wrong.

But first, some background on types and styles of interview.

....

TYPES OF INTERVIEW

> *Lap dancer Angela Cussons 24, says broadcaster Chris Evans put on her catsuit and ordered her to wear his baggy shirt and trousers. They then adjourned to a hotel where he bade her scream down the phone to impress a man friend. Later he promised her employment with his company but she was told after an interview that someone more experienced had got the post.*
>
> .   *Daily Mail*, 10 August 1998

Interviews come in many different guises. Hopefully the format quoted above is not one that you will encounter.

The primary function of an interview is to collect information. Different types of interview will look for different information:

- In a **selection interview**, the employer is collecting information about the candidate to find out if they can do the job and will fit in with the organisation. The candidate uses the interview to gather more information about the employer, the job and the organisation to decide if this is the job they want.

- In a **performance review interview**, the interviewer is collecting information about an employee's performance to identify what progress has been made so far and what performance standards can be anticipated in the future. At the same time, the employee is collecting information about the company's expectations of their performance and ways in which these expectations can be met.

- In a **development review interview**, the interviewer is collecting information to find out about the employee's potential and how this can be enhanced through training and development. The employee uses the interview to find out what the organisation can offer them in terms of development and professional fulfilment.

....

INTERVIEW STYLES

There are various types of interview in which you will take part, both in your career and your domestic life.

Structured interviews follow a set format. The interviewer asks the same questions in the same order. You may come across this type of interview if you get involved in market research, where it is important to survey the opinions of a large number of people and to present questions in a uniform manner so as not to influence the respondents' answers. Occasionally structured interviews form part of the selection process. For example, you may take part in a telephone interview as part of the pre-selection process. Telephone interviews often follow a structured format.

From an employer's point of view, the advantage with this type of interview is that it is easy to compare the information that has been gathered. The disadvantage is that it can be hard to establish a rapport between the interviewer and interviewee because there is little opportunity for real dialogue to develop.

Semi-structured interviews are less formal, although the interviewer will have a clearly defined purpose and aim. These interviews have more flexibility in the way questions are worded and the sequence in which questions are presented. Semi-structured interviews are common for both selection and appraisal.

Their strength is that they allow an exchange of ideas but at the same time maintain a recognisable format so important information can still be gathered. Their weakness is that they rely heavily on the communication skills of the interviewer, who needs to be able to listen and question effectively. Semi-structured interviews can also take up a lot of time.

Unstructured interviews encourage open dialogue. Interviewees are free to talk about what interests them, although there will still be an agenda that establishes what information must be gathered. Unstructured interviews can reveal a lot of valuable insights. Interviewees are far more likely to open up because they do not feel threatened during an informal discussion. The problem with semi-structured and unstructured interviews is that the information they gather might be hard to categorise or may be inappropriate if interviewees spend too much time wandering away from the main point. The interviewer needs the skills to prevent this happening.

✎ Think about times when you have taken part in an interview. It could be an interview:

- to get a place in college or university
- with the bank manager to get a loan
- to get a new job
- to discuss your progress at work
- to be disciplined at work
- with a market researcher who stops you on the street.

Which type of interview was it? To which type did you respond most positively?

....

THE INTERVIEWER

The success of an interview depends on more than its style and format. One of the most important factors is the interviewer's communication skills. Many interviewees make the mistake of thinking that when an interview goes badly it is their own fault. In fact, the most frequent cause for interviews not achieving their aim (to collect information) is that the interviewer is inexperienced and cannot create the right atmosphere for dialogue to take place. Bad interviewers will make you feel inferior, patronise you and sap your confidence. Small wonder you come out of the

interview room thinking that *you* made a mess
of it.

> *'I've been for interviews with power
> merchants who don't look up when you enter
> the room and generally make you feel that
> you are wasting their precious time. I've been
> for interviews with managers who hate asking
> questions and obviously want to get the
> whole process over as quickly as possible. And
> I've been to an interview where I couldn't get
> a word in edgeways because the manager
> never stopped talking about her own
> problems. There's no point in getting upset
> about a bad interviewer. The best thing you
> can do is keep your nerve and behave
> impeccably. At least then you have the
> satisfaction of knowing it is them who have
> the problem, not you!'*

If you work on improving your own interview
skills, then the risk of a breakdown in commu-
nications when faced with a bad interviewer
will be reduced. Mastering interview techniques and improving your communication
skills can put you in control of potentially
difficult situations and boost your confidence.
You may be surprised at how much difference
that makes to your performance.

Part one

THE SELECTION INTERVIEW

Hiring and firing are costly – but it's infinitely more costly to have a marginal or barely average man on the company rolls for thirty years.

Gordon W. Wheeling, *Leadership in Office*

If you associate the word 'interview' with the search for a new job, read on to find out more about:

- the part interviews play in the selection process
- types of selection interview
- the stages of a selection interview
- tests
- assessment centres.

Almost all companies use interviews as part of the process for selecting new staff. Whether you are called in to face a panel of managers and human resource management specialists in the company boardroom, spend half an hour in a small room with a flustered supervisor who asks a few perfunctory questions, or enjoy a leisurely chat over lunch with a headhunter, you are still being interviewed.

The interview is only part of the selection process. Recruiting and selecting the right staff is a complex business that can take up a lot of company time and money.

....

THE SELECTION PROCESS

Selectors go through a number of recruitment activities *before* they ask to see candidates. First of all, they have to decide where new staff fit in to their overall business plan. Are they replacing somebody who is leaving? Can the job be done by somebody else in the company? If a number of staff are being recruited, is this part of an expansion plan? How will the new recruits contribute to the company as a whole?

Secondly, the person (or people) in charge of selection compile a job description which sets out exactly what work the new recruit will take on and the standards to which they are expected to work. This helps to determine the skills and experience needed by the member of staff who will carry out the job. Accompanying the job description is a person specification which may contain a detailed list of the qualities that the successful applicant should offer.

The next stage is to look for candidates by advertising, posting vacancies on the Internet, contacting recruitment specialists or headhunters. Initial selection takes place through analysing application forms and CVs; applicants who do not have the necessary background and qualifications can be sifted out at this stage. The remaining applicants form a short list and are invited for interview.

If you are invited to an interview, you will have already successfully completed the preselection stages. You may have:

• submitted a CV

- completed an application form
- discussed the vacancy over the telephone
- taken tests
- participated in an assessment centre (a selection of tests and practical exercises).

Finding a new job is covered in detail in *Job Seeking*, also in the *Career PowerTools* series.

The interview is usually the final stage of the selection process; it is the point when you and the employer come face to face. It is the selector's chance to evaluate your skills and experience and to determine whether you are suitable to fill the vacancy. It is your chance to find out more about the company for which you think you want to work. During the interview, a lot of important questions need to be answered.

The selector wants to know:

- Will you be able to do the job?
- Will you fit in with the culture of the organisation?
- Can you develop to play a full role within the company?
- Are you the most suitable applicant compared with the other applicants?

You want to know:

- Will I be able to do the job?
- Will I fit in with the culture of the organisation?
- Can I develop to play a full role within the company?
- Is this the most suitable job for me compared to other jobs I have identified?

Notice that these questions are basically the same. Both you and the selector are looking for similar information.

It is vital that during the interview genuine answers emerge to these questions. Recruiting, selecting and putting new staff in place is an expensive business. New staff must be trained and given time to settle in. It may be some time before they become really productive or start to work at full strength, so employers cannot afford to get it wrong.

'Think about what it would cost us if we take on the wrong person. It can slow down productivity, disrupt relationships within the departments and alienate clients. It can put the whole image of the company on the line. Alternatively, a new member of staff realises this is not the job for them and leaves, so we have to go through the whole recruitment and selection process again.'

The repercussions for you if you take the wrong job are equally far reaching. You could find that:

- you are under stress because you can't do the job to the required standard
- you have problems in relationships with other staff
- you become frustrated because the job doesn't live up to your expectations
- you start looking for another job, less optimistic and self-confident than you were before.

'I thought I'd found the job I really wanted and I worked hard to get it. I was so determined to be the candidate they chose that it never occurred to me that I might not actually like the work. I didn't really listen or explore what the job involved. The

honeymoon period lasted for a couple of months. The work was much more routine than I expected and I found the atmosphere in the office very staid. Everybody sat at their desks and kept their heads down and seemed to be in fear of the managers. I began to dread Monday mornings and before long I was scanning the job pages in the newspaper again.'

So, a good interview is a vital part of the selection process, one in which many employers invest a lot of resources. Larger organisations may carry out the interview over a period of days by asking candidates to attend a residential assessment centre (there is more about assessment centre activities on pages 33–42). Even so, you will probably still take part in a more personal interview with a manager or director within the function to which you are applying.

TYPES OF SELECTION INTERVIEW

When you are asked to attend a selection interview, find out all you can about the type of interview process the company favours. You may well be given this information in the letter that makes your interview appointment. If you are not, call the company and ask. Don't make the mistake of assuming that the format for all selection interviews is the same.

Your interview could be:

- one-to-one with a manager or director

- with a panel of selectors
- sequential
- part of an assessment centre.

One-to-one interviews

If you are applying for a job with a small company, you may be interviewed by just one person, such as the managing director or the person who will be your line manager. There are some advantages to this. In a one-to-one interview you have a greater chance to establish a rapport with the interviewer and feel under less pressure to spread your attention and impress a number of people at the same time. Having said that, there are drawbacks, namely that the decision on whether you get the job or not is dependent on one person alone. That can make you vulnerable.

Interviewers are human beings, not machines. Their decisions are often subjective rather than objective. Like all of us, they have passions and prejudices and these may be reflected in the way they react to you. Specific problems you could experience in a one-to-one interview are:

- **mirroring**, when the interviewer subconsciously favours a candidate who resembles themselves in background, appearance or behaviour.
- **inexperienced interviewers** who have little grasp of how to communicate effectively
- **superficiality** when the interview is conducted with great bonhomie but at the end of the session neither you nor

the interviewer really know anything about each other.

If any of these problems become obvious in a one-to-one interview, it is up to you to take action. The biggest danger is that you will respond aggressively because you sense antipathy or apathy from the interviewer. Don't. Stay calm, keep smiling and use your verbal and nonverbal communication skills as positively as you can. Listen carefully to what the interviewer says and respond directly to their questions; don't look for inferences or try to fill in gaps in their understanding. Above all, do not let their attitude influence your behaviour. Part Three of *Interviews and Appraisals* gives plenty of advice on enhancing your communication skills and dealing with difficult situations like this.

Panel interviews

You may be asked to meet a panel of interviewers drawn from different parts of the organisation. For example, the panel may consist of someone from the human resources management function, a director, a line manager from the function to which you are applying and an administrator. Each person may be looking at a different facet of your experience or skills and, in discussion after the interview, they will make a decision as to whether or not you are suitable for the job.

In a panel interview, you are less likely to face the problems listed in the section on one-to-one interviews. On the other hand, it can be intimidating for you, the interviewee, to walk into a room in which three or four people are sitting on the other side of a large table waiting to question you.

It is good practice to acknowledge and greet all the panel members and try to spread your attention equally amongst them. Give equal weight and thought to all the questions you are asked and don't make the mistake of thinking that you only need to impress the chairperson of the panel. You need to create a favourable impression with *all* the members.

Sequential interviews

These combine both the one-to-one and panel formats. Interviewees will see a number of different staff on the same day. Each one will be looking at a specific area of your skills and experience. If you are invited to a sequential interview, you could be given a timetable that looks something like this:

Time	Interviewer	Area
2.00	HR manager	Development potential
2.30	Line manager	Skills base, relevant experience
3.00	Managing director	Career history and ambitions

In many ways, this type of interview benefits you. The decision will not be based on the opinions of one person and you will get a chance to meet with different executives and find out more about the company. The drawback is that, for the interviewee, a half day of sequential interviews can be very hard work.

Use the time during these interviews to explore fully the opportunities the company is offering and decide whether this is the job you want. Approach each stage as a separate interview and don't anticipate the reaction you will get; each interviewer may have a different agenda from the others.

Assessment centres

Many organisations, particularly those which regularly recruit large numbers of staff, now invite candidates to an assessment centre. A process rather than a place, an assessment centre consists of a variety of exercises and simulations which help to determine a candidate's ability to perform in different professional roles and integrate with other people.

Assessment centres are just one part of the selection process; if you participate successfully, you will still have an interview (or interviews) with selectors. There is a section on assessment centres explaining the activities in which you might participate (and how to approach them) on pages 33–42.

THE STAGES OF THE INTERVIEW

Interviews, regardless of type, tend to follow a set format to help the interviewer cover all the essential elements of information gathering. This is the sequence of events you can anticipate:

1. meet and greet
2. in-depth questioning
3. your questions
4. close.

1. Meet and greet

The first stage of the interview is designed to put you at ease and establish a rapport between you and the interviewer. You may exchange a few pleasantries about your journey, the weather and the cricket results – this is purely to start the conversational ball rolling.

The interviewer will briefly outline what will happen during the interview, how long it will last and what information they are hoping to obtain. By establishing these parameters at the beginning of the interview, you know what to expect. This should help you to relax.

2. In depth questioning

The second stage will begin with a discussion of your skills and experience, possibly using your CV or application form as the basis for questions. You may be asked to elaborate on past experience, to explain why you made certain decisions such as previous changes in career or to talk about your education and training.

As the discussion moves on, the scope of the

questions could change. Some selectors are less concerned about what you have done already than about what you can do now and in the future. Consequently, you could be asked to discuss how you would react in certain situations or deal with problems that arise in your work. You may also be given an opportunity to talk about what you hope to achieve as your career develops.

There is a section on interview questions and how to approach them on pages 88–91 of *Interviews and Appraisals*.

3. Your questions

The third stage of the selection interview gives you a chance to find out more about the job, your prospective employers and colleagues. Because the emphasis so far has been on the selectors getting information from you, this change in tack can be disorientating and many candidates waste their opportunity to find out more about the vacancy and the company. *'Do you have any questions?'* is all too frequently followed by, *'Er … no.'* That's a shame, because you may not have a chance at a later stage to discuss the details of the job and find out if this is what you want to do. Again, you will find it useful to read the section on selection interview questions on pages 141–158.

4. Close

Finally, the interviewer will close the meeting. You should be told what happens next, whether there is a further stage in the selection process and when you can expect to hear a decision from the selector. Then, smiles and handshakes all round and the interview is over.

So far, you have looked at interviews in which you and the potential employer talk face to face. There are, however, other formats for gathering information that employers may use as part of the selection process. These are tests and assessment centres, both of which merit more detailed examination.

....

TESTS

If the tests were rigorously applied across the board today, half of the most dynamic men in business would be out walking the streets for a job.

Walter H. Whyte, *Fortune*, 1954

The structured tests you come across when you are applying for a job are not the same as the pop psychology tests you find in magazines. The latter may be fun to complete and appear to give you insights into your character or aptitudes, but they are designed to amuse rather than provide an in-depth analysis.

Many companies now use tests as part of their selection process. Tests are rarely – if ever – the sole criteria for selection. Candidates will also take part in an interview and may also find themselves involved in a series of simulations, presentations and group discussions.

Tests used by employers are carefully developed so that they fulfil certain criteria. They should be:

- **objective** so that the information they collect is not influenced by the tester's perceptions or prejudices

- **reliable** so that you will get consistent scores even if the questions are presented at different times and in slightly different ways

- **valid** so they measure what they are supposed to measure, such as your ability to carry out a task or your skills in one particular area, like numeracy.

- **standardised** so that your score is measured against other candidates' scores. This means that your performance will be graded as high, average or low in comparison to the performance of other people who take the test. The employer may then decide that it is all the people who achieve average to high scores that they want to consider for the job.

Tests come in all shapes and sizes. Here we consider two of the most common types that job candidates experience – aptitude tests and psychometric tests.

Aptitude tests

Aptitude tests are designed to measure how suitable you are for a particular job. They can be used to measure your powers of verbal, numerical and diagrammatic reasoning. Some organisations will measure all three. Others will concentrate on aspects that are most relevant to the work you will be carrying out.

Aptitude tests are timed and you will usually find there is not quite enough time to get through everything on the paper. After the papers are collected they will be marked and assessors will compare the scores of all candidates and rank them according to performance.

Verbal reasoning tests take many forms and are designed to test a range of your skills. For example, you could be asked to:

- decode jumbled sentences
- fill in missing words
- find the odd word in a sequence
- pair words with similar or opposite meanings.

More complex verbal reasoning tests evaluate your ability to interpret the written word. You could be given a premise and asked if a number of subsequent statements follow the premise logically. You may be given a comprehension passage to read and then asked to answer questions or interpret data.

Numerical tests are equally varied, ranging from simple arithmetic to complicated statistical tables which you are asked to analyse. There are also interpretative questions which combine numerical reasoning with familiar situations – for example, you could be asked to convert currencies or work with the 24-hour clock to calculate journey times across different time zones.

Diagrammatic reasoning tests examine your spatial awareness. You may have to choose a missing section from a diagram or sequence of shapes and sizes. These are not always straightforward and could include shapes that are mirror images, inversions or rotations.

Work-related tests will reflect the sort of job for which you are applying. Some of the most familiar are word processing or shorthand tests taken by candidates for clerical jobs. You could also be asked to show that you can work with a piece of software, write a press release in a given period of time, or carry out a mechanical function using an instrument or machine.

TIPS FOR APPROACHING APTITUDE TESTS

- Read the instructions carefully before you start. Where are you supposed to write your answers? How are you supposed to record them? In a multiple choice test, do you circle the correct answer or strike out the wrong one?

- Be systematic. Start at the first question and work through the paper, don't dip in and out of different sections.

- Because time is tight, don't spent too much time on any one question. Your aim is to complete as much of the paper as possible.

- If a particular question confuses you and you can't see how to approach it, move on to the next question.

- With numerical tests, approximate the answer. Round up figures and check the multiple choice answers to see which is closest.

- With multiple choice questions, if you really don't know the answer, then guess. Unless you are told in advance that marks will be deducted for incorrect answers you can't lose any more marks by getting it wrong than you can for writing nothing at all.

Psychometric tests

Psychometric tests examine personality and aim to find out if a candidate has the right personal qualities for the job. They 'measure' qualities such as independence, leadership, and decisiveness. Employers will be able to assess such factors as your level of sociability, whether you prefer to work alone or as part of a team, what learning style particularly suits you, whether you are a leader or a follower.

Tests should be prepared by occupational psychologists and will have been extensively piloted and verified to ensure that they produce reliable, valid results. They should be selected and administered by trained assessors who come from within the organisation you are applying to or from outside agencies which specialise in psychometrics. Companies which buy in accredited tests must ensure that the staff who deliver them are carefully trained to use them properly and to give feedback. Be very wary of any potential employer who sits you down in a room and gives you a photocopied test sheet. The process should be explained to you before you start so that you understand how the tests will be used.

Psychometric tests vary in style and content. For example, you may be asked to read pairs of statements and tick the one which most reflects your way of thinking. Alternatively, you may be asked to look at lists of words and identify the ones which you think describe you. Your answers may simply consist of a tick against one of the statements, or you could be asked to score yourself on a scale of 1–5 to show how strongly you believe in what is being said.

There are no correct answers to psychometric tests. Assessors are not judging you personally, they are trying to find out if you are suitable for a particular job. For example, if you are applying for a job in sales, the employer may prefer an extrovert, self-confident personality. These are the qualities the test will look for.

You may think that you can spot a pattern in the questions, beat the system and present yourself in a particular light but, with well-constructed tests, you cannot. Consequently, the best way to approach the test is with total honesty. If, as a naturally shy person, you misrepresent yourself as gregarious, what will you gain? A job for which you are not suitable and which you will not enjoy.

Once the tests are complete and the profiles have been prepared, test administrators will discuss the results with you. Again, don't make the mistake of taking what is said personally. If you are told that your responses indicate you are better working alone than as part of a team, you are not being told you are antisocial and unfit for human company. The assessment is to establish your ability to work within certain circumstances that are relevant to the job.

TIPS FOR APPROACHING PSYCHOMETRIC TESTS

- Read the instructions carefully before you start.

- Tick the statement which most closely reflects your feelings and beliefs. Don't be surprised if the statements seem fairly similar.

- Don't agonise over your answers. Read the statements or words, tick the answer with which you identify and move on to the next question.

- Answer honestly. You have nothing to gain by trying to give a false impression of yourself.

Finally, some simple good advice. If you know that your interview will involve aptitude or psychometric tests (or both), then a few steps before you start will help you to remain calm and perform well:

- Get a good night's sleep before the day of the tests. You cannot perform well if you are tired.

- Arrive in plenty of time so that you are not flustered before the test starts.

- Make sure you have your spectacles if you need them to read.

- Listen to any instructions and ask for clarification if any aspect of the tests, however minor, confuses you.

- Read instructions carefully and do exactly what they tell you.

....

ASSESSMENT CENTRES

> *Once all first interviews are completed, we
> draw up a list for final selection. This
> normally involves a two-day residential
> assessment centre, where you'll take part in
> a range of activities such as ability tests,
> personality profiling, presentations and group
> work ... The assessors will be senior
> managers from the relevant areas of work ...
> We hold our interviews and assessment
> centres in comfortable surroundings, taking
> care to make people feel welcome. Our
> interview style is non-threatening and non-
> aggressive ... You'll be under pressure at
> times but never harassed ...*
>
> Railtrack Graduate Recruitment, 1998

Increasingly, large companies are using assessment centres to identify potential not only in
prospective new staff but also in existing
managers. Consequently, you could find that
you participate in an assessment centre either
as a job candidate or during appraisal.

An assessment centre is not a place but a
process whereby employers can look in depth
at aspects of your skills, aptitudes and personality. Where the assessment programme has
been skilfully designed it can be a helpful and
reliable way of indicating potential. So why
don't all employers use them? Quite simply,
because they are time-consuming and expensive to run and are cost-effective only for
organisations which recruit considerable numbers of staff for management positions or
traineeships.

You will attend an assessment centre together with other candidates. All the activities in which you participate will be observed either by members of the organisation's management team or by trained, professional assessors who have been commissioned to organise the proceedings and provide detailed reports on the participants.

The structure of assessment centres varies but generally they are carefully orchestrated to analyse how well you perform against criteria the employers have decided they require from their staff. For example, an organisation which is recruiting new managers may have defined a list of competences which they feel are essential or desirable in candidates for a job. These could be areas that are difficult to assess in short face-to-face interviews, such as the ability to prioritise tasks, leadership potential, decision making or negotiating skills. During the assessment centre, you will be asked to complete tasks which are designed to test these skills.

One point to bear in mind is that assessors will collate information throughout the period of the assessment centre. No single exercise is used as the sole means of establishing a particular type of skill; skills will be assessed numerous times through different activities. The matrix on the following page shows how activities might be planned for skills assessment during an assessment centre. This structure benefits you because no judgement will be made on a single activity; if you perform badly in one exercise, you may well redeem yourself in the next.

The exercises will generally be based on the job you are applying for. If you participate in

Skills area	In tray exercise	Group presentation	Role play	Individual presentation
Organisational skills	✓	✓	✓	✓
Communication skills		✓	✓	✓
Negotiating skills		✓	✓	
Leadership skills		✓	✓	

an assessment centre for a job at a bank, expect scenarios which involve financial issues and customer service. Different organisations favour different types of activity, some of which will involve a group of candidates and some of which you will complete alone. New ideas are constantly being piloted but here are some of the most common exercises you may encounter, together with tips on how to approach them.

Group discussions and presentations

Candidates are asked to work together as a small committee or team to discuss a particular problem. They may be asked to provide a tentative solution or merely to discuss the issue. Your group could be required to make a formal presentation at the end of a specified period of time. Assessors will be monitoring a range of skills, particularly how you interact with other people, your communication and negotiation skills and your ability to direct other people.

Group dynamics can play a large part in how well the objective is achieved. Theorists, notably Dr Meredith Belbin, believe that groups pass through five identifiable stages:

- **forming** – when the members get together and begin to explore personalities and review what they are expected to achieve.
- **storming** – when the group takes shape, members compete for position and test out their influence
- **norming** – when the group agrees on

how it will perform collectively and individual members find out what they can and can't do within the group

- **performing** – when the members work together to achieve the specified objective
- **mourning** – when the collective task is complete and members withdraw.

It is important within a group activity that your members move beyond the 'storming' stage to achieve a degree of harmony and begin working collectively. This may mean establishing some formal rules for the group in order to prevent certain individuals dominating the proceedings and to ensure that tasks are achieved within the given time.

TIPS FOR GROUP DISCUSSIONS AND PRESENTATIONS

- Listen carefully to the instructions.

- Greet all the members of your group.

- Keep an eye on the time so that you fulfil all the objectives of the exercise.

- Contribute to the activity as much as you can.

- Remember at all times that this is a group activity so you have a responsibility to the other members. Talk about *'we'* and *'our'* rather than *'I'* or *'my'*

- Don't dominate the proceedings – listen to the others.

- Respect other people's opinions even if you don't agree with them; avoid shouting *'Nonsense!'* even if that is what you think you are listening to.

- Use your words and your nonverbal communication signals to show that you are involved and willing to participate.

- If the discussion veers away from the matter under discussion, politely bring it back on track — point out the limited time you have to complete the activity.

Role play

Depending on the skills of the other participants, this can be great fun or absolute purgatory. Some organisations use professional actors to role play, others use their own staff. It is usually possible to tell the difference.

The simplest role plays are of the *'You are a salesperson – sell me this ashtray'* type. Alternatively, you could find yourself participating in what is almost a full stage play. You may be given a problem to resolve which involves a number of different people. You will talk to these people, listen to their opinions and their angle on the situation, discuss the problem with other members of staff and finally present your findings to the whole group.

Assessors will consider your communication, interviewing, decision-making and problem-solving skills.

TIPS FOR ROLE PLAY AND SIMULATION EXERCISES

- Play the game. This is not the time or place to take offence at being asked to make believe.

- Listen carefully to instructions and take notes if necessary so that you know what you are supposed to achieve.

- Don't make rapid judgements about the role play problem. A favourite trick is to throw in unexpected changes to the problem you are analysing so your perspective changes as you look for solutions.

- Be prepared to discuss your findings or your decisions with the assessors or the group as a whole. They will be looking for logical thought processes and solutions based on clear reasoning.

In tray exercises

This is a task which you will be asked to complete on your own. You will be given an in tray which holds a variety of correspondence, memos and other data with which you must deal. Your task is to sort through the material, prioritise tasks and decide on any action that can be taken. At the end of a given period of time, either the assessors will ask you to discuss what you have done or they may take the in tray away and look through it later. The particular skills they are assessing relate to your ability to organise tasks, to prioritise, delegate and make decisions.

TIPS FOR IN TRAY EXERCISES

- Plan your time before you start and give yourself a fixed period to read through the material before you start to work on it.

- Work systematically and read all the material before you start to prioritise.

- Make clear notes on the material of any questions you need to ask or action you want to take.

- Use headings for your notes so that the assessors understand your thought processes, e.g. 'contacts', 'action', 'refer to'.

- Don't spend too much time on any one problem; you must work through the whole in tray.

Presentations

You could be asked to make a presentation to the rest of the group. The assessors may specify the subject or you may be free to talk on any topic that interests you. You will usually be given time to prepare; for example, if the assessment centre covers a two-day period, your presentation will be scheduled for the second day but you will be told about it on the first day.

Preparation is essential if you are going to make an effective presentation. This is not an informal chat among friends, but a chance to show how well you can communicate information to an audience. Plan your topic carefully, put your thoughts in order and make notes to which you can refer when you are speaking. Use visual aids such as overhead transparencies if they are appropriate and particularly if you want to present statistical or graphical information. People remember more if they can watch as well as listen.

If you are free to choose your own subject, talk about something that interests you and for which you have a genuine enthusiasm. A topic which bores you, however worthy, will probably bore your audience. If you can select a subject that relates to the company's core business, so much the better.

Standing in front of an audience and giving a presentation can be a nerve-wracking process, particularly when you know that a lot depends on you giving a good performance. Remember that all the candidates on the assessment centre are probably experiencing the same feelings. Secondly, bear in mind the point made at the beginning of this section, that your success in the assessment centre does not rely on how well you fulfil an individual task. This presentation is only a part of the proceedings.

TIPS FOR MAKING A PRESENTATION

- Plan your presentation carefully and keep within the time limit.
- Think about your opening comments – how will you grab the audience's attention?
- Keep the format simple: tell them what you are going to say, say it and then tell them what you have said.
- If possible, use visual aids to support factual information.
- Use your voice as well as your words to generate audience interest – read the section on effective speaking on pages 126–135 of this book.
- Use nonverbal communication signals as well – smile at your audience, look directly at them, support your words with gestures.
- Make brief notes, preferably on index cards rather than large sheets of paper. Refer to your notes if you have to, but don't read them because this will make your delivery stilted.

Finally ...

An assessment centre may last over two days
and you will have plenty of time to socialise
with other candidates and staff from the
recruiting organisation. Use your self-restraint.
Performing well is difficult with a hangover.

> '*Just before I graduated, I went down to
> a London hotel for a two-day assessment
> centre. It was really enjoyable. The tasks we
> had to complete were hard work but I liked
> the other candidates and we seemed to co-
> operate pretty well. On the evening of the
> first day, we had this splendid meal with
> some of the managers, then they left us
> to our own devices. We all had to give
> individual presentations after breakfast the
> next morning so I suppose we were expected
> to go up to our rooms to prepare. Four of us
> stayed in the bar until after midnight then
> went out to a club. You can imagine the
> state we were in next morning and I still
> don't like to think how bad my presentation
> was.*'

✎ Before you move on, take a few moments
to think about your experience of
selection interviews:

- What types of interview were they?
- What was the benefit for you of this type of
interview?
- What did you think of the interviewer?
- How did their skills and level of experience
influence your performance?

....

THE INTERNATIONAL CONTEXT

So far we have considered the standard format for selection interviews in Britain. Selection processes vary across the world and their style is influenced by both organisational and international culture. It is possible to make some generalised comments about practices in other parts of the world although you need to bear in mind that these practices are continually changing as organisations experiment with new systems.

In the United States, emphasis is placed on systematic methods of selection. Tests and analysis of personality traits are much to the fore – practices that have in recent years become increasingly common in Europe. Other selection techniques include structured interviews with set questions and rating scales and assessment centres.

In eastern countries such as Japan and Taiwan, where there have traditionally been systems of lifetime employment, the selection process is very rigorous. It is important to find the right person because they will be expected to make a long-term commitment to their employer and to stay with them for many years. The emphasis is on evaluating the 'whole person' rather than merely assessing their ability to do the job. Candidates for jobs may undergo a series of interviews with the employers, managers and executives. They may also be evaluated through examinations and background checks carried out by investigators who talk to their neighbours and acquaintances and check out police records and family history. If this sounds rather far fetched in its thoroughness, it is worth remembering that parts of the British Civil Service operate in a similar fashion when recruiting new staff.

Interviews appear to be a common feature of selection worldwide. What varies are the other methods used with the interview to complete the selection process. Western countries, or those influenced by their management practices, tend to favour psychometric testing, assessment centres and group selection methods.

Having considered the interview as part of the selection process, read on to find out more about a second type of interview in which you may regularly be involved – the appraisal interview.

Part two

APPRAISALS

> *Appraisals are where you get together with*
> *your team leader and agree what an*
> *outstanding member of the team you are,*
> *how much your contribution has been*
> *valued, what massive potential you have*
> *and, in recognition of all this, would you*
> *mind having your salary halved.*
>
> Guy Browning, *Guardian*, 1995

Appraisal systems vary according to the culture, size and resources of an organisation. Most companies do, however, have a systematic method of evaluating staff performance and many include a formal interview as part of this process. Part Two of *Interviews and Appraisals* looks at:

- some examples of appraisal systems
- the stages of the appraisal process
- appraisal interview styles.

There is nothing new about the concept of performance review. Employers have always assessed performance and looked for ways to improve it. Robert Owen, who owned textile mills in Scotland in the early 1800s, is a prime example. He had a system whereby a multicoloured block was placed above an employee's machine. The colour on the front of the block showed what the supervisor thought about the previous day's performance. Some organisations in China still use a similar system today.

The twentieth century move towards more 'scientific' management methods made employers think more carefully about working practices and how they affected productivity. Output-based and objective-based approaches gained popularity, particularly in the United States. The emphasis on employee output stimulated interest in appraisal techniques. Since the 1940s, the practice of performance appraisal has spread across the world. This is partly due to the growth of multinational corporations which operate appraisal systems at headquarters and implement these in all their factories and outlets. It is also due to the increased interest in management theory; research into business and the development of new management systems is now a massive industry and has generated many new approaches to working practice (of which appraisal is one) that organisations adopt.

So, when you go through the appraisal process you are really doing nothing original. The approach your managers take may appear innovative but the principle behind appraisal is well established.

Typically, an appraisal system will be used to serve a number of different purposes:

- to monitor how well staff are performing in their jobs
- to increase motivation and improve job performance
- to determine training and development needs
- to identify 'high flyers' who merit promotion
- to help with decisions on allocating pay rises and other rewards.

Companies differ in the ways they assess staff, although almost all will have some way of finding out what you are doing and what you can achieve in the future. You may have an appraisal interview every six months in which you discuss your performance to date, set objectives for the next review period, discuss what you personally want to get out of your job and find out whether you merit a bonus or a pay rise. Alternatively you may have separate interviews to review your performance, your potential and your rewards. Just to add to the lack of uniformity in modern appraisal techniques, you will also find that:

- some companies use different terminology for what is essentially the same thing. For example, one company may refer to *development reviews* and another will talk about *potential reviews*
- there are numerous different systems for appraisals involving different people acting as assessors
- appraisals may be carried out by some companies every three months and in other companies only once a year
- some companies favour open appraisals where assessments are disclosed to the employee. Others use closed systems and do not allow staff to see the results of their assessment.

Consequently, this book concentrates on developing the skills you can use in all types of appraisal interview rather than focusing on a particular system. Having said that, it will be helpful for you to understand the most common systems and what they aim to achieve.

....

APPRAISAL SYSTEMS

Appraisal systems bring together the needs of three different parties:

- the individual
- the manager
- the organisation.

Theoretically appraisals enhance communication between these parties and ensure that they are working towards common goals. Appraisals usually fall into one of the following three categories (although as we have already said, they might have different names):

- performance review
- development review
- reward review.

Performance reviews

These assess your performance over a given period of time. The objective is to control and enhance your performance and to ensure that your objectives complement those of the company as a whole. The performance review is intended to maintain and improve standards of work and will address a number of different issues, such as:

- how you have performed so far
- how any problems you experience can be addressed
- whether you have met any objectives set during previous reviews

- what performance objectives you should meet during the forthcoming review period.

One familiar method of performance review, popularised by management guru Peter Drucker, is management by objectives.

Management by objectives provides a system which is easy to monitor and lets everybody know just where they are. The employee has specific targets which they must achieve and these will usually relate to some outcome that can be quantified. During appraisal, previous objectives will be reviewed to see if they have been met and new objectives will be set. It is a system which many companies have adopted because it gives a clear focus to employees.

There are some problems with the system, however. You cannot control every factor of your working life and your ability to fulfil your objectives could be compromised by external factors. Secondly, the appraisal becomes very results orientated. This may be good for the company but it pays little heed to the needs of the individual who is being assessed.

Development reviews

These relate to career planning and focus more on you, the employee. Again, they may look at what you have done in the past and at your current performance but they will also consider where you want to go next. What do you, as an individual, hope to achieve in your career? How can the organisation contribute to your development and at the same time, improve its own productivity? In a development review your manager acts as your coach and supporter, looking for ways to enrich your job and develop your potential. The focus is on you as an individual, although obviously there will be a payoff to the organisation if you are fulfilled and continually developing in your career.

Your manager may use the development review to identify gaps between the skills you use to do your current job and additional skills you need to acquire to carry out your next job. For example, if you work in sales, your next step up the career ladder might be to become a section supervisor and then a section manager. Your manager can determine the training and development you will need to fulfil these new roles.

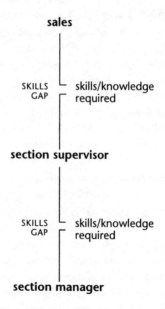

sales

SKILLS GAP — skills/knowledge required

section supervisor

SKILLS GAP — skills/knowledge required

section manager

Skills and knowledge gaps can be addressed in a variety of ways, such as:

- training
- secondment
- work shadowing
- job rotation
- committee work
- project work
- mentoring.

By identifying specific shortfalls, you and your manager can source the most appropriate method of extending your experience so that your development is part of a focused plan.

Reward reviews

These determine rewards and benefits for employees. Here we are not just talking about the increase in pay and the company car, but also increasing the power, status, sense of fulfilment and freedom employees experience.

Whether the three different types of review are assessed through a single appraisal interview or separately through different interviews depends on your organisation's approach. One major problem that arises if employees have a combined appraisal interview to review performance, development and reward is that the purpose of the interview can get confused. Performance reviews focus on the organisation and how you meet its needs. Development reviews look at you and how you can achieve your personal and professional goals within the company. Managers who have to cover both areas at the same time may find it difficult to combine roles which involve assessing (and sometimes casting judgement) on performance and encouraging an open discussion of your future. Also, performance reviews often demand discussion of fairly minor detail whereas a development review may take in much wider issues. Thus, within the thirty minutes or hour allotted to the interview, too much ground has to be covered.

THE APPRAISAL PROCESS

The appraisal process is cyclical and follows four stages, as shown in the figure.

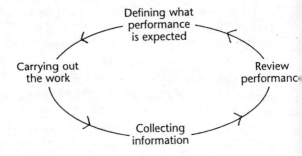

1. Defining what performance is expected

During this stage, you agree with your manager what the organisation wants from you and what you are expected to achieve. This could include setting certain standards of performance that you should meet and defining precise targets relating to your work.

2. Carrying out the work

Once the objectives are defined, you can work towards them. You may have informal meetings with your manager to check your progress and for your manager to collect and record information on how you are performing.

3. Collecting information

Towards the end of the formal appraisal period, your manager will collect the relevant information to use at the appraisal interview. This information can come from a number of sources.

Downward appraisal is the most familiar system. Line managers supervise their staff and produce objective assessments of their performance before the appraisal interview. Line managers are well placed to understand the work of their staff and to develop realistic performance objectives with them.

The manager carrying out the appraisal may complete a form which asks specific questions such as:

- How far have the agreed objectives been achieved?
- What strengths/skills contributed to this achievement?
- What aspects of performance need improvement?

Self-appraisal asks you to produce an assessment of your own performance to compare with your manager's assessment. You are asked to identify your own strengths and weaknesses and may be asked to answer such questions as:

- What part of the job do you think you do well?
- What objectives were agreed for this review period?
- What hindered your performance or the achievement of these objectives?
- What steps can be taken to overcome these problems?
- What training support do you need to improve your performance?

These questions are not easy to answer. If you are by nature shy and reticent, then promoting your own achievement may be difficult. Similarly, if you feel that your performance is hindered by a colleague, how do you communicate this without sounding like a petulant child? The answer is that most people stick to the middle ground and say very little. Help with this kind of situation is given in Part Three of this book in the section on negative feedback (pages 172–180).

Upward appraisal occurs in some larger organisations. It is often a part of a varied appraisal system that involves staff at many different levels. Quite simply, employees give their views on how well their superiors have performed. It is a good idea in principle, though it demands a lot of trust between all parties. This system has been used mainly in the United Kingdom and United States, although some organisations in South Africa, Canada and the former Soviet Union have also introduced it.

Peer appraisal is useful when people work in a team. Information on performance is submitted by all members of the team and they review each others' contributions. This system is not yet widely used since peers tend to be reluctant to evaluate each others' work. Nevertheless, peer judgements have been shown to be reliable in their accuracy.

Customer appraisal is becoming increasingly important as customer service takes a priority role in many organisations. Customers are asked to rate the quality of products and service and these ratings are linked to the overall appraisal of the employee's performance.

360 degree appraisal combines appraisal from all the above sources. This method provides the most thorough appraisal and gives a rounded view of how an individual staff member performs. It is particularly useful for evaluating the performance of top level managers who may have few people in senior positions to their own who could carry out a performance review. Three hundred and sixty degree appraisal has many positive aspects. It is comprehensive and therefore difficult to ignore: you may feel justified in disregarding the opinions and evaluation of one person but an assessment from a number of different sources is hard to overlook. It can help employees perform more effectively because they see how their actions impact on a wide range of people, and it increases understanding of how staff need to work together. On the other hand, 360 degree appraisal is a very time-consuming process that can lead to a heavy increase in paperwork. Another drawback of involving too many people in the appraisal process is that some will be unwilling to give honest feedback, particularly on the work of their superiors.

As you read through these options, one major obstacle to the more detailed appraisal systems may have come to mind. If you move away from the traditional downward appraisal system where a single manager appraises the performance of a staff member, the amount of information that must be collected, recorded and analysed increases dramatically. All this takes time and the system can rapidly become unwieldy and unworkable – particularly if it must be carried out every six months.

Once information is collected, it has to be recorded. Again, there are many different systems in use. Some of the most common are:

Norm-referenced appraisals, which compare an individual's performance against the other members of the group. This gives a rank to each employee and the manager has a list which compares how team members have attained specified targets, rather like the ranking you may have got in class at school.

Behavioural appraisals consider employees individually and don't compare them to each other. This method of recording information may use rating scales to create an overall picture of performance. Managers complete a form which asks them to grade an employee's performance, e.g.:

  presentation skills   1 2 3 4 5 (where 1 is high)
or
  presentation skills   high   average   low

This is an easy system to implement but it is not always an accurate reflection of performance. It is very subjective and thus may say as much about the appraiser as the appraisee. The manager may tend to mark everybody as average rather than make more extreme judgements. There is also a risk of the 'halo' effect influencing decision, where you mark somebody you like too high and you mark somebody you don't get on with too low.

The other difficulty with these scales is that although they may highlight weaknesses, they don't offer any advice on what to do about them. If your manager grades your presentation skills as low, which particular aspects should you improve, and how should you go about making that improvement?

4. Review performance

This is the appraisal interview itself. Both you and your manager will have something to say and the aim is to reach agreement about what has been achieved. Then you will decide what will be achieved in the next appraisal period by defining and recording performance targets, setting out what you are expected to do next. Thus the whole process has started once again.

Appraisals should involve a structured recording system whereby what is agreed is written down. This means that both you and your manager are clear about the action you should take next. If your organisation operates an open appraisal system, you will see this report. There should be a copy for both you and the manager and one kept in your personnel file. In a closed appraisal, you will not see the documentation. The records may well form part of the basis for the next appraisal interview along with any self-appraisal material you have been asked to complete.

Formal appraisal will be held at fixed intervals but in the interim period you may have informal 'check-ups', such as weekly meetings with your manager, team meetings or coaching sessions. These informal sessions give both of you a chance to deal with minor problems as they arise and stop the formal appraisal interview getting diverted into a discussion of small details.

....

PROBLEMS

One problem with a formal appraisal system is that many employees cannot see how it is a part of their regular work. It is an annual or six monthly event that they prepare for and benefit from at the time, but a few days later they forget about it. It does not really impact on their daily routine.

Managers often take the same attitude. For

them, appraisal can be a time-consuming interruption to their usual work schedule that involves a series of unpleasant tasks, namely in-depth discussions with staff and mountains of paperwork.

A second problem arises in companies that use one appraisal interview to combine both performance and development reviews. If, for example, your company operates a system of performance-related pay and this is discussed in the same session as your personal development objectives, then your manager is both helping you and judging you. To fulfil two such different roles at once is difficult. And it may be hard for you to be honest about your needs or weaknesses if you think that any admission of infallibility could damage your pay packet!

Ideally, a performance review will be followed closely by a separate development review so that the manager can ensure that objectives can be met and there is no skills gap that will impede progress.

....

APPRAISAL INTERVIEW STYLES

Having briefly considered different review systems, it will help you to get the most out of the process if you understand something of the way in which we communicate during appraisal interviews. Next we consider different styles that managers can use when they enter into discussion about your performance or development. In Part Three of *Interviews and Appraisals* you will find a lot more information about communication skills, including how to interpret and respond to different questioning techniques.

During a formal appraisal interview (or in the course of your daily work), you may be called in to discuss particular tasks that your manager wants you to achieve. Your attitude towards these tasks will be determined by a number of factors such as your interest in the task, how you think it will benefit you and how your manager approaches you.

In some professions and cultures, giving and taking orders is a routine part of work and individuals would be uncomfortable if anything other than a direct instruction was given. It would be difficult to introduce a caring, sharing, 'let's discuss this fully and make sure we are all happy' approach when you are asking a platoon of soldiers to go over the top to certain death.

Psychologists and management theorists, however, have spent a lot of time analysing what makes people want to work and meet the objectives set by their bosses. This is a complex field but what has emerged is a belief that, in general, autocratic styles of management can be counterproductive. Workers who are involved, fulfilled and feel that their managers take a genuine interest in them and what they do, perform better than workers who are treated like machines. Consequently, the way in which managers communicate their wishes to their staff is very important.

In 1958, the American psychologist Norman Maier highlighted three styles of communication between managers and their staff:

- tell and sell
- tell and listen

• problem solving.

Look at how these styles might be used during an interview to set work-related objectives.

Tell and sell

A manager tells you how your performance has been judged and then gains your agreement that this judgement is correct. The manager also sets the objectives and sells them by presenting them so forcefully – or persuasively – that you accept their decisions.

You've probably come across this style. Your perception is that you are being led through the conversation and, although you may have a chance to interject, your opinions don't carry much weight.

> *'The IT training has gone really well. Now we need to look at communication skills. If by the date of the next review you can prepare a report on external training providers, then we'll be able to get the courses up and running by the end of September. That's going to help everybody.'*

It may be that you agree with what your manager is saying but this style of delivery gives you little control over what happens next. By stressing the advantages for the organisation as a whole, your manager has ensured that any protest on your part puts you at a disadvantage; it implies that you are not pulling your weight for the team.

Tell and sell is one-way communication. It can make you defensive and unwilling to comply with future objectives. So how can you deal with a manager who favours this approach?

One tactic is to have your evidence to hand. If you need to resist something that is being 'sold' to you, then you need to present valid and watertight reasons. Secondly, you need to be precise about *why* you are objecting; this avoids any implication that you are simply being uncooperative.

> *'I think that you are absolutely right. We need detailed research into training providers for the communication skills course. But there are an awful lot of them and I want to make some valid comparisons into cost and provision to make sure we get the very best. Could we look at dates again so that I have time to prepare a thorough report?'*

Tell and listen

Your manager tells you what they think and then asks for your opinion.

> *'If you prepare a report on external training providers for the communication skills course before the date of your next review, we could get the course up and running by September. How do you feel about that? Do you think that is a realistic time scale?'*

This method involves you more directly and gives you a chance to make an active contribution *providing* you really believe that your manager is listening and acting on your response. If you feel that they have already decided on what will happen and are merely putting forward an instruction in disguise then, once again, you may feel defensive and cornered.

It does, however, give you the chance to put your opinions forward. If you have prepared your arguments, you can be more confident that your viewpoint will be accepted.

'I'm happy to prepare the report and I realise we need to get the information together as quickly as possible. At the moment, though, I'm working on the recruitment and selection project for next year's graduate intake and that will take up a lot of time during the next two months. I think it would be more realistic to set the target for the communication skills training report for the beginning of October.'

Problem solving

This encourages the manager to act as a counsellor and encourages you to identify problems and set solutions.

'Can you use any of your experiences in organising the IT courses to help establish the communication skills course? For example, how do you think we can get the research into external providers underway?'

Using a problem solving interview style can be a powerful motivator, stressing your owner-ship of the problem and making you *want* to contribute and take action rather than com-pelling you. Your opinions are just as impor-tant as your manager's and you are in a position to negotiate deadlines and detailed objectives that are acceptable to you both.

These defined and recognised styles are not the only situations in which you can find yourself during an interview where you are negotiating objectives and targets. Depending on your manager's style and awareness of interviewing techniques, you could also find yourself in an interview that uses a very autocratic style, where you are simply told what you have achieved and what you must do next.

> *'You've handled the new IT training courses successfully. Now prepare a report on external training providers for communications courses and let's get those up and running by September.'*

What can you do with a manager like this? Your agreement is taken for granted. It may be worth pointing out any misgivings you have although you cannot necessarily expect them to be acted upon. At the same time you must put your reservations forward in such a way that your willingness cannot be questioned.

> *'I'll be pleased to prepare a report. Can we agree a time frame for getting the information together because I want to do a thorough job?'*

Equally difficult to handle is the interview in which your manager expects you to do all the talking. This approach places all responsibility firmly on your shoulders and can leave you feeling lost and unsure of your direction.

*'How did you get on with the IT course?
What do you think comes next?'*

Some managers would argue that such an approach puts the employee in charge of their work and thus empowers them. Unfortunately it also gives you no guidance. You don't know what your manager wants, or how your work fits in with their own targets.

In a situation like this, you may have to take the initiative. Use the opportunity to highlight what you want to achieve next and take a problem-solving approach yourself to draw the manager into the dialogue by asking their perceptions.

*'I learned a lot through organising the IT
course, particularly about the range of
training providers. There are so many of them
that I think it is important we carry out
detailed research before we set up any more
courses. That will take time. What I would
like to agree with you is a programme for the
next six months to see how we can fit in the
research and schedule the courses. What time
frame did you have in mind?'*

All these scenarios demand that you take a positive approach. You will not always agree with the targets that are set for you but these can be changed *providing* you use your negotiation skills. What you cannot afford to do is:

- say no without having a watertight reason for your refusal
- agree half-heartedly, then go away and forget to do the work
- appear resentful or mutinous. Such an approach immediately sets up

communication barriers between you and your manager that can have lasting repercussions.

In part, the success of your interview is dependant on the skills and experience of your interviewer. An interviewer who is trained or is adept at listening, questioning and analysing information, will make the appraisal process more productive than a manager who does not possess, or refuses to practice, good interview skills.

A good interviewer will use a combination of questioning techniques to encourage you to open up and will make sure that you have a real dialogue and not a one-way conversation. A good interviewer will also use factual evidence, avoid making personality judgements and will remain positive.

It is up to you to participate in a similar manner, to be willing to share your thoughts and feelings and to accept feedback as a positive contribution to improving your performance rather than as an implied criticism on your performance.

One way to improve your understanding of the many different ways we negotiate targets is to put yourself in your manager's shoes. It is easy to criticise a manager for taking an autocratic approach or not involving you sufficiently in discussions and disregarding your needs. But how would you perform if you were the manager and it was your job to agree objectives?

✎ Take some time now to think about the approaches you use when you are discussing targets or objectives. These need not be work-related. We are all involved in negotiating objectives in every aspect of our lives. Put yourself in the position of the person who wants to get the work done in the following situations. How would you set the targets and negotiate or persuade the other person to comply?

1. You want a junior member of your department to spend two days a week for the next month clearing out the archives.
2. You want a colleague to help you introduce a quality audit system for customer service.
3. You want your partner to agree to install double glazing.
4. You would like the bank manager to advance a loan for this double glazing.

TIPS FOR APPROACHING APPRAISAL INTERVIEWS

- Ask your manager or human resource management department to clarify how the system works. Find out the frequency and format of appraisal interviews and whether they will be performance or development reviews (or both combined).

- Recognise that the appraisal interview is intended to help you, not to criticise you.

- Remain objective and listen to what the appraiser says.

- Be willing to accept advice and look for constructive ways in which it can be put into practice.

- Review your performance and aspirations before the interview and make notes of the salient points you want to make.

- Take ownership of the appraisal process; this is your career that is under discussion.

THE INTERNATIONAL CONTEXT

The systems we have described above are largely based on western organisations and their perception of appraisal and how it can work. Appraisals are practised across the world but they may have a different purpose or emphasis. It is worth being aware of the cultural context, particularly if you work for a multinational corporation which has offices across the world. Head office in London or New York may set the policy for appraisals which are carried out in Bangkok, Nairobi or Mexico City. Can the same systems and approaches be used in all three places? The answer is, quite simply, no. Not if you want to get an accurate impression of how staff perform and of what they are capable.

In many Pacific Rim countries, the manager is still seen to take a paternalistic role towards staff and this is reflected in appraisal style. Appraisals are used to coach, guide and develop employees. Much of this guidance may be informal, since in medium-size organisations there is less reliance on a human resource management function and more on the manager as leader and guide. A major difference between the western system of performance appraisal which focuses on how well you complete tasks and 'do the job' and the system in Asian countries is that in the latter there is greater concern for the 'whole person' and the way in which they fit the organisation. Consequently, appraisals consider aspects of personality, something which is not encouraged in western meritocracies.

For example, in China, achievement of objectives is important and is often related to bonuses and performance-related pay. At the same time, great emphasis is placed on dependability and loyalty to the organisation so the individual's performance may be appraised on different levels.

Successful appraisal systems demand a high degree of openness between all parties and for everyone involved to speak honestly about strengths and weaknesses. The great respect given to those of senior age or social status in some countries, particularly in Asia, can restrict the openness of appraisals. It would be very difficult for a young manager to appraise the performance of an older subordinate who works in a relatively junior position. Difficulties of this kind also arise in societies which place a heavy emphasis on 'face'. Face means maintaining both one's own and another person's self-respect. To openly criticise, or to infer a criticism, can destroy 'face' and cause resentment.

Too much praise can raise equally complex dilemmas within the organisation. In Japan, people tend to work in teams and may dislike being singled out for extra responsibility since this breaks the harmony of the group. Thus, changes to the existing system (such as moving somebody into a supervisory role) must be justified to the whole team. Managers are expected to give detailed guidance and instructions about what they anticipate their staff will accomplish.

Cultural differences impact on appraisal interview styles. In Korea, appraisal systems are in place but they are concerned largely with counselling and development since career advancement is based mainly on seniority within the organisation. Negotiation plays a far less important role than in western societies and employees expect to 'listen and be told' rather than make a strong contribution to the appraisal process. When it comes to setting objectives, these need to be given clearly and precisely as they will be fulfilled exactly.

It is always dangerous to make too many assumptions about practices in other countries but one point is evident: appraisal systems and the way in which managers handle them are not consistent across the world. Any manager who works in a country other than their own, or any employee who is posted overseas, would benefit from studying the purpose of appraisal, the attitude towards staff who are in a management or supervisory role and the communication styles of the country in which they work. If they do not, they run the risk of inadvertently creating disharmony through using methods that are inappropriate.

In this part of *Interviews and Appraisals* you have considered different types of appraisal systems and some of the communication styles you could encounter during an appraisal interview. There has been guidance as to how you can deal with some of the situations you encounter during such interviews. But to really perform well in any sort of interview, you need to think carefully about all your communication skills and how you can use these to optimum effect. That is what you will go on to do as you read Part Three of this book.

INTERVIEW SKILLS

The first two parts of *Interviews and Appraisals* set the scene by looking at selection and appraisal interviews, the career-related interviews in which you will be most frequently involved. The third section looks in greater detail at the communication skills you will use during these interviews.

If you take up tennis, you do not go onto the court for the first time expecting to qualify for Wimbledon. You expect to learn the techniques of the game, hone your skills and practice until you are a competent player. The same principle applies to interviews. By thinking about what you have to do during an interview (for example, presenting a positive image to a selector, answering questions and receiving feedback) you can work to improve your skills in these areas. The more confidence you have in your interview technique, the more you will achieve during a face-to-face meeting. Refining your interview skills frees you to concentrate on the dialogue with the employer rather than worrying about things you might be doing badly.

Part Three of this book looks at a broad range of skills you will use during both selection and appraisal interviews, specifically:

- preparing for interviews
- presenting a positive image
- nonverbal communication
- using your voice
- listening
- questioning techniques
- receiving feedback.

Finally, there is a short section on how you can monitor your progress after the interview. If you are looking for a job, this will help you to maintain the momentum of your job search. For appraisals, it will show you how to integrate the appraisal interview into the whole appraisal process and thus develop a more systematic approach to monitoring your career.

In Part Three, you will also find the Golden Rules. These offer simple, straightforward advice to improve your interview technique. They are brought together and summarised at the end of the book.

....

PREPARING FOR A SELECTION INTERVIEW

GOLDEN RULE 1

You cannot expect to perform well in an interview unless you are adequately prepared.

For most work-related tasks we expect to have to do some preparation. Interviews are no exception. So, how do *you* prepare for a selection interview? For that matter, do you prepare at all, or are you one of those candidates who believe that getting a job is in the lap of the gods?

Thorough preparation for an interview will build your confidence and help you avoid the hazards that so often contribute to poor performance. It helps you give a good account of yourself. Why, then, do so many job candidates limit their preparation to checking the date and time of the interview and skimming through their CV just before they leave home?

> *'I think a lot of people are very fatalistic about job interviews. Their attitude seems to be that getting the job depends on external factors, not on themselves. They spend a lot of time worrying and getting themselves into a state before they go, but they don't seem to realise that there are actions they can take to improve their performance at the interview and improve their chances of getting the job. I can always tell which candidates have prepared for an interview and which haven't.'*

Fatalism is fine if you prefer to believe that your life is not under your own control. If, however, you take a more proactive approach then you will understand the importance of spending some time and effort on getting ready to meet your future employers.

You started to prepare for the selection interview when you submitted your application form or CV. That was the preliminary point of contact when you expressed interest in working for the organisation and presented the reasons why the selectors should consider you.

If you are called for interview, you have already successfully cleared the first selection hurdles. A lot of other candidates have been rejected; only a small number of applicants will be called in to meet the selectors. You have already dramatically improved the chances of getting the job.

Now you need to prepare for the final hurdle, the interview itself.

How much do you know about the organisation?

GOLDEN RULE 2

Research the organisation, the job and your ability to fulfil its requirements *before* the selection interview.

You should have already carried out some research into the organisation you wish to join. If you haven't, then start immediately. Showing a selector that you took time to find out about the company's work and the market in which it operates indicates that you are serious about wanting to work for them.

Find out all you can about the organisation's:

- products and services
- philosophy and mission statement
- financial performance
- management structure
- competitors
- directors and senior management
- locations and numbers of staff
- training and development programmes.

Finding this information is not difficult. You can consult:

- business directories and trade registers
- market research such as Mintel and Key Note reports
- company accounts and reports
- promotional and marketing literature

- company histories
- Web sites on the Internet.

The employer may send some company literature to you when they invite you for interview. Otherwise, ring up and ask for it. Explain what you want and ask that it is sent to you as soon as possible. If you work or live nearby, volunteer to go in and pick up the material yourself; this will give you a chance to look at the company's premises.

Large organisations often provide a wealth of information, from recruitment hints to detailed analysis of their products, markets and organisation.

The Internet is a particularly useful source of information. Even small companies now have their own web sites and many of these will include copies of company reports and accounts. You may also get profiles (and pictures!) of members of the management team.

> *'I don't expect candidates to know everything about our organisation, but I get a bit impatient with those who haven't done their homework. We have a huge web site which we refer to in our recruitment literature. An hour spent looking at that will give a recruit a good idea of what we're about. If you want to work here, surely you can invest a little time finding out who we are.'*

You can get valuable information from friends and colleagues who either work for, or know somebody who works for, your target company. But take hearsay for what it is: other people's opinions. Try to stick to the facts. We are all guilty of occasionally making negative comments about our work and these cannot be taken as an accurate reflection of what our workplace is really like. Just because your next door neighbour's daughter-in-law says that she worked for the sales director at XYZ Engineering and thought he was aggressive and inconsiderate does not mean you have a reliable view of the company culture. And never, ever, quote something you have heard during an interview. If your comments are inappropriate you will do yourself no favours and you may start a witch hunt for your informant.

Finally, don't forget your local library. The reference section will carry up-to-date business directories or know where you can find these and many city and county libraries now operate business information services which will help you find out about specific companies and areas of employment.

How much do you know about the job?

Hopefully, you will already have a detailed job description which came with your application form or pack. If not, then ask for one. Providing job descriptions is a standard task in most organisations, although you may still find that smaller or less formal companies do not have anything written down. In that case, telephone the company and ask to speak to somebody who is familiar with the function or job for which you are applying. Make it clear that you need information *before* your interview and ask for a written outline of the main responsibilities to be sent to you. Such a request is perfectly reasonable. You cannot talk intelligently about a job during an interview unless you know what that job involves.

Look closely at the job description. Ask yourself:

- How many of the responsibilities it lists are familiar?
- What areas are new to me?
- What parts of the job excite or challenge me?
- What parts of the job do I feel will be most difficult?

Now look at each of these in turn.

Familiar responsibilities

During the interview, provide evidence that you can successfully tackle these aspects of the job. Think about similar situations in your current job and come up with examples that support your claims to be competent in this area. For example, if the job description cites: 'assisting the section leader in developing new accounts', look to your experience in developing new business in your most recent job. Think of two occasions when you have brought in new customers or developed systems to increase sales.

New responsibilities

These provide a challenge and should be part of the reason you want the job. Use them positively. You may not have had experience in a particular field but that is no reason why you should not be recruited for the job. Emphasise that these are areas in which you want to extend your experience and skills.

Research training opportunities that could support your work. For example, a job description might state that you will be required to give presentations and pitch for accounts as part of a team. You may not have had the chance to do this in your present role, but you can highlight the fact that you have watched and helped others prepare for presentations, that you are aware of the need for good presentation skills to succeed in this job and that you would hope to receive coaching and training to improve your own skills.

The challenge

Why do you want this job? Look at the job description. What challenges does it offer that you will not get elsewhere? It is these factors that you need to identify and use during your interview. The selector hasn't written the job description for fun, but to outline areas of responsibility that are important to the organisation. If you can demonstrate enthusiasm and a willingness to take on new areas of work, then you are presenting a positive attitude on which an employer can build.

The difficulties

No new job will be absolutely perfect. Neither are you. There may be areas in which you are inexperienced or which you don't relish having to deal with. If these are mentioned during an interview, how do you tackle them?

Perhaps the best advice comes from an experienced selector:

> 'If somebody tells me that this job is just what they want in every way, then I find it

*hard to believe them. Every job has elements
that are frustrating, boring or problematic.
Those elements have to be addressed during
an interview just as much as the challenges
and opportunities. I would rather a candidate
is honest and admits that they may find
some parts of the job hard. We can address
their problems together and look for solutions.
A candidate who is not willing to admit some
shortcomings during interview may not be
willing to do so when they are working – and
that can cause problems for everybody.'*

Be honest but be positive. There is a big
difference between refusing to do something
or pretending a problem does not exist, and
saying: *'I don't particularly enjoy that part of the
work but I appreciate it has to be done and will get
on with it'.*

How much do you know about yourself?

You may not know yourself as well as you
think. In a life packed with activity and
change, you cannot possibly remember everything you have done. Some of the things you
have forgotten about may well be relevant to
the job for which you are applying.

Having researched the organisation and
analysed the job description, now turn your
attention to yourself. Look at your CV or the
copy of the application form you sent in for
the job. What skills and attributes does the job
require? What parts of your experience are
particularly relevant? What evidence can you

produce to show that you are the right person
for the job?

Spend some time matching up what you
can offer with the requirements of the job.
Break down the job description under headings like the ones in this chart. The most
important heading is the final one. What
evidence can you produce to support any
claims you make about your ability to do the
job? It doesn't mean you have to come up
with remarkable, world changing achievements; straightforward examples of everyday
work can be just as effective. Look at this
example and then try the same exercise for
yourself.

Job description asks for	Good communication skills
My skills/ attributes	Communicate (verbally/in writing) confidently with staff at all levels
My evidence	• Customer service team leader • Written reports for sales director • Three years in telesales

Sometimes, you will find evidence when you
really don't expect to. Work that you carried
out some time ago, small tasks that you took
care of, day-to-day routine that you scarcely
think about – these can all provide examples
of your ability to do the job well.

'I applied to take on additional responsibility for record keeping in my school. I came up with some ideas before the interview but I didn't get the post. Afterwards we were debriefed and I discovered that the other candidate had made suggestions that were very simple and basic. So basic that it never occurred to me to include them even though they were practices I followed in previous jobs. Her attention to detail convinced the selection team she was the right person for the appointment.'

How much do you know about the interview?

Do you know what type of interview to expect? Are you going to meet a single selector or a panel? Is it a single meeting or sequential interviews with different personnel? How long will the interview last? Will you be expected to take any tests while you are there? Will you have a chance to look around the premises and meet other members of staff?

You may have received answers to all these questions in the letter inviting you for interview. If not, find out before you get there.

Confirming the format of the interview and knowing what to expect will keep you calm and in control. You do not want any surprises that will unsettle or unnerve you when you walk into the interview room. And there is nothing more unnerving than thinking you are going in for a cosy chat with one selector and finding yourself faced by a panel of four interviewers, each of whom has a list of prepared questions.

If you are not given sufficient information about the interview format, then ask. Make a list of questions, then telephone the selector or the human resource management department and ask for the answers. Find out:

- how long the interview will last
- how many interviewers you will see
- whether it is a sequential or panel interview
- the name(s) if possible. (Remembering names is extremely difficult when you are introduced at the beginning of the interview, particularly if you meet more than one interviewer)
- if you need to bring anything with you (certificates, portfolio, etc.).

Similarly, if you have been invited to attend an assessment centre, you may be able to find out some information beforehand, such as:

- how many candidates are attending
- whether the assessors are from within the organisation or from a professional recruitment organisation
- how long the assessment centre will last
- the type of activities that will be included (they may or may not be willing to talk about this).

Preparing questions

GOLDEN RULE 3

Many selectors ask similar questions so you can think about your responses before the interview.

There is a section later on questioning techniques. This will help you understand what interviewers are doing when they ask you particular questions. Read it carefully. The more you understand about the way interviewers operate, the more prepared you are to meet their requirements.

> *'It was the simplest question of all – 'Why do you want this job?' And I'm damned if I could think of what to say.'*

As you prepare for the interview, spend some time thinking about the questions you could be asked. That does not mean you need to prepare scripted answers, merely that you should have thought carefully about what you want to say and how you will tackle standard questions should they arise. (You will find a list of frequently asked selection interview questions on pages 155–157.) How will you expand on the points you have made in your CV or application form? Remember that key word *evidence*. Make no claims that you cannot substantiate.

You should prepare some examples of ways in which you have dealt with specific challenges or problems at work. The 'Tell me about a time when …' question is very popular with some interviewers since it makes you talk at length. That sort of question is fine providing your mind doesn't go blank. Make brief notes about times when you:

- worked on a major project with your colleagues
- led a team of staff or directed a project
- dealt with a problem

- introduced a new business practise or innovation to your department
- completed a job or project that gave you great satisfaction.

For each of the above, outline:

- what happened
- who was involved
- how you tackled the issue
- how you felt about the issue
- how you would act differently if a similar situation arose again.

By clarifying events in your own mind, you are better prepared to give a coherent and concise account to an interviewer.

You also need to think about the questions *you* want to ask. In their enthusiasm to prove themselves and get the job, candidates sometimes forget that the interview works both ways. The selector is assessing your suitability for the job but at the same time you should be weighing up the company and the job to find out if it is really what you want.

As the interview progresses, you will learn a lot more about both. Be prepared to ask questions to clarify any details about which you are unsure. Before the interview, work out what you want to know about:

- the job
- the staff
- the organisation's culture
- the organisation's direction and plans for the future
- reporting systems
- appraisal systems
- reward systems
- reward packages

- opportunities for promotion
- training and development.

Be precise. Ask *'What will I be working on during my first few weeks?'* rather than *'What general responsibilities will I take on?'*

Don't be afraid to ask difficult questions if you really need to know the answers. For example, you may want to know what happened to the previous job holder or to find out whether the company has high or low levels of staff turnover. Such questions are not impertinent providing you have good reason for asking them rather than just idle curiosity.

Many structured and semi-structured interviews leave time for you to ask questions at the end. By all means take advantage of this opportunity. Even better, filter your questions into the conversation throughout the interview. It is more natural, particularly if you have developed a rapport with the interviewer, and makes the whole process less interrogatory.

Check the details

GOLDEN RULE 4

Leave nothing to chance and check the details of your interview.

So far you have considered the essential fabric of the interview, the dialogue that will take place between you and the selector. You also need to take care of the minor details to make sure that your visit to a potential new employer runs smoothly. The more prepared you are in every aspect, the easier you will find it to concentrate on the business of the interview itself.

You know the date and time of the interview but do you know where it is to be held? If you are visiting a local company that should not be a problem, but if you are going out of town or to another part of the city, then you need to be absolutely clear on the directions. 'Take the tube to Leicester Square and it's across the road on the corner – you can't miss it', is fine in theory until you get to Leicester Square underground station and realise it has more than one exit. And an awful lot of corners on the other side of the road.

When you confirm the interview arrangements ask for clear directions and a map, if one is available, then estimate how long it will take you to get there. If possible, and your interview is in the same town or city, make a practice run a couple of days beforehand. If you have to go out of town, plan your journey. Travel by train rather than risk rush hour traffic and, if the appointment is early in the day, consider travelling the day before and staying overnight. Your aim is to arrive in plenty of time so that you remain unflustered. Getting to the venue 15 minutes early will give you time to prepare yourself, check through your CV and focus on what you are about to do.

If you do have a few minutes to spare and are asked to wait in reception, remain on your best behaviour. You may be observed when you don't realise it. Don't smoke, sprawl across the chair or take a short nap. If there is some reading material lying around, look at the company brochures rather than a copy of the *Sun*.

'I thought I'd given myself ample time to arrive at the interview but signal failure held up the trains and I got there twenty minutes late. The interviewer was very understanding and told me not to worry about it, but arriving late completely threw me and I know that I didn't give a very good account of myself. Now I'd advise anybody to set off at least an hour earlier than they need to. If you do arrive early, find somewhere nearby to have a cup of coffee. Anything is better than being late.'

Secondly, plan in advance what you will wear for the interview and what you need to take with you. Your clothes say a lot about you and dressing appropriately is important. It gives a positive first impression to the selectors and it builds your confidence to know that you look good. There are sections on dress and grooming on pages 109–115. Select your clothes the day before the interview and make sure that they are in good shape. Discovering a mark on your tie or a button missing from your jacket just before you leave the house is more than a nuisance, it is yet one more thing that can put you off balance.

If the interviewer has asked you to bring along documentary evidence such as certificates and diplomas or part of your portfolio, put all these together the day before the interview, not at the last minute.

Finally, if your journey to the interview location involves any walking at all, take an umbrella. It always rains when you don't want it to.

TIPS FOR PREPARING FOR INTERVIEW

• Do your homework – find out all you can about the job and the company.

• Familiarise yourself with the interview format so that you will not be caught off-guard if asked to do something unexpected.

• Think about questions you might be asked and how you will answer these.

• Think about questions you want to ask the employer.

• Give yourself plenty of time to travel to the interview venue so you arrive punctually.

....

PREPARING FOR AN APPRAISAL INTERVIEW

GOLDEN RULE 5

Appraisal is a two-way process that demands input from you as well as from your manager.

Depending on the system your company uses in carrying out appraisals, you may take part in an interview with your manager that:

• reviews your performance throughout the past few months
• sets targets for the forthcoming review period
• considers the direction your career is taking, and
• identifies areas for professional development.

Alternatively, you may attend separate interviews. One will be a performance review and will focus on what you have achieved and what you should focus on during the next review period. The second will be a development review that determines where you are going within the company and how you will get there.

Making adequate preparation before the interview (regardless of whether it is performance review, development review or a combination of both) will help you to get the most out of the process. Thinking about the process and what you want to clarify with your manager extends the degree of control you have over the whole appraisal process. It builds your confidence and will help you determine how your career can develop in the way that suits both you and the company.

Time and place

Your manager should give you plenty of notice before the interview is due to take place so that you have time to prepare. The appraisal interview is an important part of anybody's career calendar and can't be carried out on the spur of the moment when you both have a few minutes to spare. You should also know how long the interview will last. Make sure that you have organised your diary so that you have sufficient time, plus a little to spare if the interview runs over.

Where will the interview take place? Ideally, the setting for the appraisal interview will encourage discussion rather than a sense of being tested. Many managers prefer to use comfortable chairs in another part of the room rather than sit behind their desks. The setting for the interview should be both private and quiet. Confidentiality is an important part of the appraisal process and it is difficult to discuss issues openly if you believe somebody else in the organisation can eavesdrop from their desk outside the door. There should also be minimal interruptions. You want to feel that your manager is focusing on you, not on outside calls or other people's problems.

Once you know when and where the interview will take place, think about what you want to discuss with your manager. Start by assessing your own performance during the review period. You should have any notes from previous appraisal interviews that set out targets you agreed last time round. You also need to look through your daily log book to refresh your memory about events that have influenced your performance during the review period.

Keeping a log book is a key feature in monitoring your performance at work. You don't need a complicated, lengthy document but you do need to keep a record of day-to-day events. For more about setting up and maintaining a log book, read the section on monitoring your progress after an appraisal interview on pages 184–188.

Ask yourself the following questions and make brief notes of your answers:

- What have I done well?
- What could I have done better?
- Which objectives from the last review have I achieved?
- What evidence do I have of those achievements?

• What do I want to achieve next?

It is important to be honest when you answer these questions, particularly when it comes to looking at what you can do better. None of us is perfect and however well we perform in our work, there will always be room for improvement. It is these areas that you need to identify both for your own benefit and for that of the company.

Don't be too modest. If you think that there are achievements you have made that deserve recognition, then state them. Hopefully your manager will be aware of your achievements, but if there is something you think they have missed out, bring it to their attention during the interview. Far better that you state your case clearly than you are resentful afterwards because you feel aspects of your work are being taken for granted or going unrecognised.

At the same time, avoid overplaying your hand by exaggerating what you have achieved. Taking credit for something and implying that you were the only person involved when your manager knows it was a team effort will do you no favours. Identify your specific contribution to the team effort and state that.

Objective setting

GOLDEN RULE 6

Contribute to your appraisal interview by setting your own objectives.

Setting objectives or targets that you should

achieve within the forthcoming review period is a joint effort. How *your manager* defines those targets will be influenced by:

- what is happening in the business now and in the coming months
- where the business is going in the longer term
- budgets and resources
- previously agreed objectives and how well those have been achieved
- what you, as a member of staff, want to achieve.

How *you* define those targets will be influenced by:

- your success in achieving previously defined targets
- your workload
- your short-term ambitions – what you want to achieve professionally during the next year
- your long-term ambitions – the overall direction of your career.

Hopefully these objectives will dovetail so that you and your manager can agree a plan that is acceptable to you both.

Setting objectives sounds easy. You and your manager both decide on what you want to achieve and plot a course of action. You define certain tasks that must be completed within a given time frame then you go away and get on with it. So why do so many people find that at the end of a review period, the objectives they set previously have not been achieved?

The problems arise because of the difference between what we *think* we can do and what we *actually have the time and energy* to achieve.

There is often a gap between the two. This happens in every part of our lives, not just at work.

Think about it. You wake up on Saturday morning and mentally list all the tasks you need to complete during the day. You schedule them as you drink your first cup of tea: walk the dog, go to the supermarket, wash the car, mow the lawn, visit your mother, catch the football in the afternoon ... The dog takes off after a rabbit and takes more than an hour to recapture, the supermarket is packed with people and it is after midday before you finish the shopping. You wash the car but before you can start on the lawn, the rain comes down ... By the end of the day you are exhausted by the frustration of not achieving what you set out to achieve.

This scenario is not unrelated to the sort of situations you face at work. The objectives seem clear-cut when you discuss them with your manager but achieving them is another matter. The workplace is not consistent, things do not always work to plan. You find that the 'best laid plans of mice and men ...'

One way to deal with the difficulties of achieving objectives is to be more systematic in your approach to setting those objectives. Many managers believe that the best way to go about this is to get SMART.

You may well have come across SMART in other areas of your work; it is a commonly used system for defining and setting objectives. The acronym suggests that any objective should be:

- **specific** – it should be very clearly defined so that everyone involved knows exactly what has to be achieved. Objectives should be related to a specific area of the business such as productivity, financial performance, business development or service quality

- **measurable** – you should be able to measure whether you have achieved your objectives either by completing a certain quantity of work, meeting specified quality targets or completing the work within a defined time scale

- **attainable** – objectives should be challenging enough to stimulate you but you should know that you can achieve them. If your targets are over ambitious, they put you under stress and you may stop trying to achieve them

- **relevant** – the objectives should match up with the overall objectives of the company and should be relevant to your job

- **timed** – in line with the need to define objectives precisely, they need to be timed so you know how long you have to meet your targets. Some objectives may be short term, others may cover a longer time span.

Using SMART to analyse every objective can be time-consuming and will over complicate matters. However, you can take the basic principles and apply them when you are thinking about what you can achieve. This will help you to design objectives that you and your manager can agree and that you can achieve without too much difficulty.

If this sounds simple but you have doubts about how it works in practice, read the following case study. It looks in some detail at how Jennifer, an employee in a printing company, set realistic objectives to improve her working routine. As you read, think about how Jennifer's actions can be adapted to your own situation.

CASE STUDY: JENNIFER

Jennifer is the office manager for a small printing company. During the last six months, she has experienced a number of problems in her job. Recently, new software was put onto her computer but there has not been sufficient time or resources to train her to use it. Jennifer is picking up the basics as she goes along and doing a reasonably good job but she is aware that she is not using the system to its full extent and she finds that frustrating. Mastering new techniques is slowing her down and making her anxious – if anything goes wrong, she has to find someone else to sort it out.

Her second problem is her relationship with senior management. Although she deals with day-to-day administration and accounts, she feels that she has little responsibility. She is not consulted about the way in which the office system is organised. She wants to increase her involvement with the company as a whole and not to be seen as 'just the office manager'.

Basically, Jennifer is rather bored. She works for a reputable organisation, she gets a good salary and benefits package and she likes her colleagues. Her day-to-day routine is varied but the weeks and months are slipping away and increasingly she wonders what will happen next. She cannot see any scope for promotion within the company because the organisation is quite small. Although she is not hooked on climbing the career ladder to reach the heady heights of a directorship, she would like to think she was going somewhere …

Every year, Jennifer has a formal appraisal interview. It is not something she looks forward to. She sees it as a necessary evil, a time when her bosses check up on her, look for new ways to use her skills – and increase her workload. To Jennifer, the appraisal process is one that benefits her bosses. She has yet to see that she can use it to her own advantage.

Jennifer can use the appraisal interview to her advantage if she takes time to prepare. By taking steps to examine her own situation and think about what she wants to achieve, she can identify objectives that would relieve her present problems. By having a clear sense of direction she improves her chances of developing an action plan that will suit both her and her employers.

Jennifer needs to develop objectives that contribute to the development of a workable career plan. To do so, she needs to bear certain points in mind:

- **She should aim for steady improvement in her situation and not a quick fix.** A job is a sum of its parts and improvements in specific areas may prove more beneficial than trying to bring about major change.

- **She must accept that she and her managers are working together.** If she is fulfilled in her work, then her performance will improve and she will not be tempted to seek employment elsewhere.

- **She needs to think constructively about ways to improve her situation** and see the appraisal process as a means of achieving what she wants.

Jennifer could use a four-step plan to define her own objectives before the appraisal interview. By knowing what she wants, she will be better placed to negotiate realistic objectives with her manager. The four-step plan is one that you can adapt for your own use.

Using the four-step plan

1. Identify three things that you want to achieve

Think about your working life as it is now. What do you want to achieve? These could be changes designed to alleviate immediate problems or changes that affect the direction of your career in the long term.

In Jennifer's case, the three things she wanted to achieve were:
- mastering the new software
- greater involvement with the company administration as a whole
- a chance to widen her skills base and gain more recognised qualifications.

2. Prioritise these three areas

You cannot achieve everything at once so you need to prioritise. This may not be easy because all three are important. Ask yourself what aspect of your work do you most need to change at the present time?

Jennifer decided that mastering the new software was most important because it would remove the pressure that was affecting her daily routine and increase her confidence. Secondly, she wanted to begin some formal training to improve her skills base. Interestingly, her desire to get more involved with management was the least pressing of her concerns.

3. Establish precise objectives for each area of change

Trying to make major improvements in all three areas will achieve little since your personal resources will be spread too thinly. Take the first of your priorities and focus on that. Look for ways in which you can develop an action plan to implement improvements.

Jennifer's first priority was to master the new software. She wants to understand how the system can be best used within the context of her own work. She particularly wants to apply the system in VAT operations and to improve data management and thus speed up the processing of invoices. She can measure how well she achieves this objective by setting a time frame for improvements, for example by deciding that she will have the system under her control by the end of the next VAT accounting period. Her objectives are realistic and attainable; she knows that with help and training she can master the system.

Next, Jennifer looked at ways in which she could get the help she needed to achieve this objective. She wanted time to examine the system and she needed tuition from somebody who was proficient in its use. The software company which installed the package could offer tuition on site and would send a trainer in at the company's convenience.

4. Show how your objectives can benefit your organisation

Your objectives have to complement the company's business plan and overall development strategy. You need to be able to 'sell' what you want to your employers.

As part of her action plan, Jennifer presented the following information:

Objective	To master the new software package
Benefits to employer	Improved efficiency, data processing will take up less time thus freeing me for other work
Benefits to me	Improved efficiency, greater confidence, more time to get involved with other functions such as personnel
Suggested action and timing	On-site training for two weeks followed by off-site support course for one month. Monitor progress after training by comparing times for invoice preparation
Resources needed	External trainer to be brought in to the company for one hour per day for intensive tuition for a two-week period. During training, my work will be covered by another member of staff

Jennifer has clearly defined what she wants to achieve and is now in a strong position to negotiate with her manager. Her preparation did much to build her confidence and to make her feel that she was an active contributor to the appraisal process. Her manager also benefits from her participation because he has a clearer idea of what Jennifer wants from her work and what she feels she can cope with.

✎ You can try this process for yourself. Think about your responsibilities and workload as they are now. Break down major issues into specifics. Rather than generalised statements such as 'I'm overworked and can't get through everything that is expected of me', look at what exactly you are expected to achieve and list your daily actions. Which of these are really important? Then follow the four step plan:

1. Identify three things that you want to achieve or change.
2. Prioritise these three areas.
3. Establish precise objectives for each area of achievement.
4. Show how your objectives can benefit your organisation.

Yes, it takes time and no, it is not always possible to deal with all work-related issues so logically. But by following the process, you are spending time thinking about your work, the challenges and dilemmas you face and the ways in which you can improve your daily routine. Time spent focusing on such issues is never wasted.

TIPS FOR PREPARING FOR AN APPRAISAL INTERVIEW

- Don't forget that you and your managers are working together.

- Aim for a steady improvement in your situation and a measured increase in your responsibilities.

- Be proactive and identify your own objectives.

- Follow logical steps in defining these objectives; look at timing, resources, benefits for both you and your employers.

- Keep your own records, such as a log book, to record what you are achieving and what problems you face.

....

PRESENTING A POSITIVE IMAGE

| GOLDEN RULE 7 |

Your appearance tells the interviewer a lot about you.

___

Appraisal interviews will usually take place with somebody you know reasonably well so this section of *Interviews and Appraisals* (which considers aspects of self-presentation) is more relevant to those attending selection interviews. Having said that, presenting a positive image at work is important to everybody, not just job seekers. So make use of the advice if you feel that you need to.

Like it or not, the way you look counts. Your

appearance sends out strong messages to others about:

• the way you see yourself
• the way you want others to see you
• your willingness or unwillingness to conform to social expectations.

Interviewers often make judgements within the first few minutes of meeting you, long before you have had a chance to say anything constructive. Those judgements will be based on your appearance and your nonverbal communication signals such as posture, facial expression and the tone of your voice.

The problem with initial impressions is that they are difficult to modify. If we respond positively to somebody when we first meet them, perhaps because of the way they look, we will go on liking them. Similarly, negative first impressions tend to endure. Ask yourself how many times have you congratulated yourself on how accurately you 'summed up' a new acquaintance: 'I knew from the start he was ...'

The way you dress and your grooming play a major part in creating the first impressions that can influence a selector's attitude towards you. Research into the effect of clothing suggests that we respond more positively towards those who are formally dressed and tend to follow their lead. Hence the generally accepted belief that one should dress smartly for work. It has also been suggested that our clothing conveys distinct messages about our social and economic position, education, background, level of sophistication, moral character and trustworthiness!

*'I took a cheap flight on an airline where
the cabin staff wore jeans, trainers and
sweatshirts. The service was fine but it didn't
feel right. They looked so young and casual,
I kept wondering how they would cope if
there was an emergency.'*

Of course, first impressions can be misleading
and there are notable business successes who
flout the conventions and sport sweaters and
trainers in the board room. But to do that
takes great self-confidence and a conviction
that one's personality can overwhelm other
people's perceptions and beliefs. For most of
us in business, appearance is a tool that we can
successfully use to create a rapport with colleagues if we play by fairly conservative rules.

Clothes

*Many a man has busted in business because
his necktie did not match his socks.*
Frank McKinney Hubbard, *Epigrams*

We live in a style conscious age. Whether you
feel it is necessary or not, you may sometimes
need to replace clothes that still have some
wear in them. The suit you have worn for
interviews since you graduated in 1982 may
no longer be serving you well. Outdated
clothes do little to reinforce an image of
dynamism and cutting-edge business sense.

Fashion is notoriously fickle. For women,
the changes are particularly difficult to keep
up with. A couple of years ago, brown was the
new black, then purple became the new
brown that was the new black ... then black

became the purple that was the brown that was the black. Skirt lengths go up and down faster than an escalator in an underground station. Trouser widths, necklines and shoe heel designs change at dizzying speed. Men are not immune to these changes, either. The width and design of your tie, the size of your collar and lapels all reflect your style consciousness. That's how the fashion industry makes money.

That does not mean you have to spend a fortune on new clothes every time you attend an interview. A few well-chosen, classic styles are a good investment and will prove useful for a reasonable period of time. Spend your money wisely and focus on that word 'classic'. Look for clothes that are simple and will not date when fashion enters a new cycle next year.

Your aims when you dress for an interview are to:

- feel comfortable with the image you present
- engender confidence in the people you meet.

You will do this by wearing clothes that you like but, unless you are a true individualist who can carry off the unusual with aplomb, a smart, well-groomed, classic style will give you the self-assurance to meet people at all levels with confidence. In turn, the first impression you make on those you meet will be of somebody who is sure of themselves and takes time and trouble over their appearance. Quite simply, you need to look smart. This list gives a few basic ground rules:

Smart dressers choose	Smart dressers avoid
Well fitting clothes	Clothes that are too tight, too short, too loose
Simple styles (suit, jacket and trousers or skirt)	Fussy styles
Toning colours	Loud, clashing colours
Comfortable clothes	Restrictive clothes
Classic styles that don't date	Radical fashion
Clothes that mean business	Dressing for leisure or clubbing when they are going to work

If you are working in another country or with colleagues from another culture, respect their dress code. Dress is often tied to cultural and religious concerns; flouting the conventions shows a lack of respect and a degree of arrogance that will gain you no friends. Standards of modesty, particularly for women, vary enormously from one country to another and you would be wise to find out what these standards are if you are working away from home. For example, in some countries in the Middle East it may be acceptable for women to wear shorts and a skimpy T-shirt on the beach but in the streets and at work they should cover their knees, shoulders and neckline.

In hot, humid countries like Malaysia, dress codes are as formal as they are here although they have been refined to cope with the climate. The batik shirt, which can be worn without a tie may be acceptable for the office but wearing any other sort of shirt without a tie is not! Ask what is expected of you and always follow the lead of your local colleagues.

Grooming

GOLDEN RULE 8

If you care about yourself, you will care about the business.

Good grooming is common sense and should be something we practise all the time. It is surprising, therefore, how many people still turn up for interviews looking unkempt and uncared for. And the British have a particularly bad reputation for 'self-maintenance'.

Grooming is not just a question of style. It encompasses a key question that employers must address: if you cannot be trusted to take care of yourself, can you be trusted to take care of business? This question becomes even more important if you are involved in a customer-focused industry where the image you present to the general public reflects that of the company. If you are an adult, in control of your life and thus able to take on a responsible job, then that degree of responsibility will be reflected in your grooming.

Good grooming is about consistent maintenance, not spending large amounts of money. You do not need a full facial, manicure and three-hour session with the hairdresser before an interview. What you do need is to spend a little time getting ready.

Good grooming means	Good grooming doesn't mean
Tidy hair	Dandruff!
Polished shoes	Down at heel, scuffed shoes
General cleanliness and freshness	Heavy perfume, stale smelling clothes
Clean hands and nails	Grubby, bitten nails
Discreet makeup	War paint!
A briefcase/attaché case	Carrier bag
Clean shaven or a trimmed beard	Five o'clock shadow
Minimal jewellery	Glitter
Clean, well-pressed clothes	Grubby collar and cuffs, crumpled clothes

TIPS FOR CREATING A POSITIVE FIRST IMPRESSION

- Manage your appearance in the same way you would manage any other project – plan, take action and review.

- Try on the clothes you plan to wear the day before the interview. Don't leave it to the last minute to find that your skirt or trousers no longer fit.

- Avoid fabrics that crumple, such as pure linen. They may be stylish but they rapidly look creased and unkempt.

- Carry an umbrella to deal with the uncertainties of the weather.

- Take a spare pair of tights or a spare tie. If

you don't, you are almost certain to ladder the former or spill something on the latter.

- Beg or borrow a briefcase if you need to carry papers.

- Leave your anorak at home. Invest in a decent coat or raincoat.

- Check the minor details, such as the state of your shoes and fingernails.

- Get your hair trimmed regularly. Don't leave it to the last couple of days before the interview unless you are absolutely sure that you will be happy with the results.

If you have doubts about your dress sense and personal style, or feel that you need more guidance, then put your pride to one side and ask for help. Talk to friends whose appearance you admire and ask them for advice. Alternatively consult the professionals. There are plenty of organisations that will analyse what suits you, restructure your wardrobe, help you choose new clothes that complement your colouring and generally make a positive difference to the way you look. Their services may not be cheap, but they could prove a sensible investment.

'I went to pitch for some work with a small publishing company. I wore a suit, as I always do when I'm visiting an oganisation for the first time. The managing director wore faded, ripped jeans, a denim shirt and a lot of jewellery – as did most of his staff. Yes, I might have felt comfortable if I had been wearing the same sort of casual uniform but I'm glad that I didn't. I applied the same standards I always apply to interviews

and that gave me confidence. And yes, I got the work.'

....

NONVERBAL COMMUNICATION

GOLDEN RULE 9

Everything you say can be reinforced or undermined by your nonverbal communication signals.

A man walks into an interview. He looks vaguely around the room and sits down hesitantly. He blinks continuously, doesn't look directly at the manager on the other side of the desk. His attention seems to be focused on the floor. His hands are clenched in his lap. Every few seconds he touches the side of his face.

'Now,' the interviewer thinks. 'I wonder what he's got to hide.'

'Oh God,' the man thinks, 'my contact lens is stuck in the corner of my eye.'

Thousands of pages have been written about nonverbal communication. It is a major area of research, and justifiably so. It has been estimated that the human body is capable of more than 270 000 gestures and they all mean something. Less than a third of what we communicate is through the spoken word. More than half of your message is conveyed through your body language (stance, facial expression, gestures, etc.), more than a third through your tone of voice and less than 10 per cent through your words.

Nonverbal communication signals emanate from our subconscious; they are powerful because they are less controlled than the words we speak. No wonder nonverbal communication is such a rich area for exploration. The problem is that, like this manager, we may be misled because we believe we are experts in nonverbal communication when we are not.

During an interview, the way you present yourself is very important. Your stance and posture, your gestures, can communicate messages very effectively. Awareness of some of the principles of nonverbal communication can be a great asset because it could prevent you from giving negative signals. At the same time, becoming too involved in the interpretation of nonverbal communication can be counterproductive because it makes you self-conscious and you will no longer concentrate on everything else that is going on during the interview.

So, be aware that a little knowledge goes a long way. And never forget that not everyone gives the same nonverbal communication messages. The person who huddles in their chair may be cold rather than afraid of you. The woman who does not wish to shake your hand is not necessarily rejecting you; she may come from a culture where physical contact between men and women is frowned upon. And the man who taps his foot continuously, thus irritating you and making you wonder why he is so nervous, may be totally unaware of what he is doing.

Your aim in an interview of any kind is to

create a positive impression. Most people, when they are interested and enthusiastic, do this automatically. We are all giving out non-verbal communication signals all the time and we rarely think about it.

✎ Think about these two examples:

- *Next time a friend walks into the room watch yourself and consider how you greet them. You may rise slightly from your chair or incline your body towards them. You may put out your hand towards them. You will probably smile and look directly at them. The only word you use is hello, but your body says that you are pleased to see them.*

- *How do people show that they don't want to meet you? Make a list of negative nonverbal communication signals that could be used by somebody who is trying to ignore you.*

Messages are communicated through a combination of nonverbal signals. On the following pages we look at some of these, particularly:

- eye contact
- posture
- gestures.

Eye contact

The term 'eye contact' is a misnomer. When we maintain what is known as eye contact we are directing our gaze towards the top half of the other person's face, not staring directly into their eyes. However, it is the commonly accepted term for focusing on the person with whom we are speaking.

Eye movements are among the most expressive and most frequently used nonverbal communication signals. Your eyes themselves change according to your mood. When you are interested in someone, your pupils dilate; when you are bored or distracted they will contract. In western cultures, maintaining eye contact shows interest and a willingness to listen. Allowing your eyes to wander around the room suggests that you are bored. Looking at the ground or away from the other person can signal that you have something to hide. It is worth remembering that these guidelines do not apply in all societies. In some parts of Asia and the Middle East, it is customary to look down or away when talking to a superior to show respect. Neither is it expected for women to look directly at men. To force eye contact in situations like this would be both discourteous and embarrassing.

During an interview, keeping your eyes on the interviewer not only shows that you are interested and paying attention but will also help you concentrate on what is being said. If you are in a panel interview, avoid focusing on just one person even if he or she may seem to dominate the proceedings. Spread your eye contact around all members of the group and look at each one as they speak.

Your eyes can be used to signal a range of responses. Lifting the eyebrows and slightly widening the eyes can indicate that you wish to speak without you having to interrupt with words. Most people will pick up on this and let you interject. Similarly narrowing your eyes can show suspicion or discomfort.

Eye movements are rarely used in isolation. As you widen or narrow your eyes, you may be nodding or shaking your head. You will reinforce a message by not only maintaining eye contact but also by gesturing with your hands and changing your posture.

Posture

'The way somebody walks into the room is very important. Obviously, you don't make assumptions about their character purely on that, but it is yet one more thing that contributes to the overall impression they make. Nervousness is to be expected at the beginning of an interview but I look for people who make a positive effort to overcome that nervousness. I have a lot of respect for the person who puts their shoulders back, holds up their head, takes a deep breath and walks confidently into the room. If they can do that with me, then they can do it with our clients.'

When you want somebody to listen to you and to take notice of what you are saying, how do you position your body? If you are standing, you may well push your shoulders back, raise your chin and stretch your spine. If you are sitting, you might push your body further back in your chair so that your head is raised. Probably without thinking, you are making yourself look taller and projecting your physical presence and, in turn, your voice.

The way somebody sits and stands can

communicate something about the way they feel and their intentions. An upright posture, in which the head is raised and the chin lifted, denotes confidence and assertiveness. Hence the importance of posture for soldiers; a slouching army with its collective eyes cast down to the ground would hardly inspire confidence in its followers or fear in its enemies.

When you walk into an interview, your posture is one of the ways in which you set the tone of the proceedings. If you stand straight and look the person you are meeting in the eye, you signal confidence. If your shoulders are hunched and your head droops, you give the impression that you are nervous. The interviewer will subconsciously process these signals along with all the other nonverbal messages you give and use them to build that initial impression that counts for so much in the way we relate to each other.

Your posture when you are seated also makes signals. Slouch in a chair as you would when you are at home relaxing in front of the television, and you look as if you are unconcerned about what is happening. Perch on the edge of the chair and you will look alert but you may also look as if you are very nervous and about to take flight.

In an interview with somebody you have not met before, such as a selector, your posture should signal that you are closely following everything that is being said. Sit upright with your back firmly against the back of the chair; this will help you keep your head level and slightly raised. If you are a 'fiddler', prone to fidgeting with your hair or biting your nails, then keep your hands in your lap or on the arms of the chair unless you are actually using them to emphasise a point of speech.

In an interview with somebody you know reasonably well, such as your manager during an appraisal, your posture will probably be more relaxed and open. Men, particularly, tend to range themselves across a chair when they are talking to somebody they know with their arm across the back of the chair, body in a semi-reclining position, legs outstretched or loosely crossed. Such a posture indicates that you are confident and can talk openly with the other person.

Your posture will change as the conversation progresses. You want to make a point so you lean forward. Somebody says something that amuses you and you lean back. These are all part of the communication patterns we use to accompany – or replace – words.

Gesture

I do not object to people looking at their watches when I am speaking. But I strongly object when they start shaking them to make certain they are still going.
Lord Birkett, the *Observer*, 1960

If we accept the premise that all those thousands of gestures we make mean something and we consciously began to monitor what we are signalling, we would rapidly become so obsessed with our nonverbal communication signals that none of us would dare leave the house. Rather than start analysing what particular gestures can signal, let us concentrate on practicalities. What signals should you avoid because they might irritate or communicate a negative message to the interviewer?

Fidgeting, making unnecessary and repetitive movements can be very irritating for the person on the other side of the table or desk. Tapping your fingers or a pencil, constantly pushing back a lock of hair, jiggling your foot, picking at a hangnail are all gestures that you are probably not aware you are making. For the person you are talking to, these movements can begin to dominate everything you say and do. They are more than irritating habits; they can also signal extreme nervousness or impatience. Equally, folding your arms and keeping your head lowered suggests that you are nervous or, even worse, have something to hide. You are giving the impression that you do not want to be in the room and that is not a positive basis for any interview or meeting.

The problem is that for many people, these are habits which we have maintained for so long we are no longer conscious of them. Breaking a habit you don't recognise you have is more than a little difficult, but it can be done.

Gesture can, of course, be used positively. Hand movements reinforce what we are saying. Think about it. You might raise your hands, palms upwards to signal that you are open minded about something or you don't know the answer. You might count on your fingers as you talk through a list of items. Such gestures, together with your stance, your facial movements and your words, work together to create an impression of total participation in the conversation. Again, beware of the line between using gestures positively and over-doing it. Waving your hands around like a windmill, pointing directly at somebody or clenching your fists when you talk are all negative signals.

✎ This checklist can help you to evaluate the sort of nonverbal signals you give to other people and to help you put a check on those habits that can prove irritating. In the first column there is a list of common nonverbal signals. In the second column, put a tick for yes and a cross for no to show whether or not you give each of these signals. In the third column, make a note of anything you want to change or improve upon. If you are serious about improving your nonverbal communication signals, photocopy the checklist and ask a trusted friend to fill it in to show what nonverbal communication signals they have seen you make. Compare their answers with your own.

Signal	Yes/no	Change/improve
APPEARANCE		
dress appropriately for the occasion		
dress casually all the time		
POSTURE		
stand straight		
sit upright		

continues on the next page

Signal	Yes/no	Change/improve
sit back in chair		
folded arms		
hands on hips		
head up		
shoulders slumped		
EYE CONTACT		
look at other person		
eyes down		
eyes roam the room		
VOICE		
loud		
soft		
fast		
slow		
hesitant		
'um', 'er', 'OK'		
GESTURE		
pointing		
waving hands		
fiddling with jewellery, hair, etc.		
tapping feet		
cracking knuckles		
hand over mouth		

continues on the next page

Signal	Yes/no	Change/improve
EXPRESSION		
frown		
nervous smiling		
biting lips		
clenched jaw		
scowl		

TIPS FOR IMPROVING YOUR NONVERBAL COMMUNICATION

- Don't get too obsessed about nonverbal communication signals or you will become self-conscious.

- Keep your stance relaxed but upright when you are walking, standing or sitting. Shoulders back, head up, stomach held in.

- Avoid irritating gestures. Keep your hands loosely folded if you don't need to use them.

- Look at people when you are talking to them.

- Ask a trusted friend to tell you if you have any irritating habits you should correct.

....

USING YOUR VOICE

GOLDEN RULE 10

Use your voice as well as your words to
engage and keep the interviewer's attention.

It is not just your nonverbal communication
and your words that count in an interview.
The way you use your voice is important too.
Your voice is a powerful tool which, with a
little care and attention, you can use to your
advantage.

Your voice communicates through:

- pitch and tone
- speed
- volume
- use of pauses
- disfluences (*'uh'*, *'er'*, *'OK'*, etc.).

Along with your nonverbal signals, your voice
gives your listener clues about what you want
to say. Even if you listen to someone speaking
in a foreign language that you don't understand, you can often tell by the tone of their
voice something of what they are feeling,
particularly if they are angry, sad or excited.

Some people are easier to listen to than
others. We are aware of 'good' and 'bad'
speakers. Those we enjoy listening to are
generally people who modulate and change
the pitch of their voice and vary the speed of
their words. They are, quite simply, more
stimulating to listen to. 'Bad' speakers may
deliver their words in a monotone or are hard

to hear because they speak too quickly or their pitch is too low.

> *Success depends on three things: who says it, what he says, how he says it; and of these three things, what he says is the least important.*
> John Morley, *Recollections*

There is no such thing as the 'ideal voice'. What we find attractive in someone's speech pattern or voice is influenced by our culture. In some societies, speaking rapidly and loudly is good; in others, a good speaker is soft and slow.

This table shows what makes the difference (in western societies) between voices that are easy or difficult to listen to.

Easy to listen to	Difficult to listen to
Modulated pitch	Pitch too high Pitch too low
Moderate speed	Very fast speech Very slow speech
Clear projection	Very quiet speech Very loud speech
Varied tone	Monotone

Nervousness can cause problems when you speak. If you have ever had to give a presentation or speak in public you will be familiar with the overwhelming physical reactions you can suffer. Your mouth becomes dry, you fear that when you begin to speak nothing will come out and, to your own ears, your voice sounds either timid and too quiet or very harsh.

It is true that when we are nervous, our voice changes. Adrenalin can cause the throat muscles to tighten and raise the vocal pitch. We also tend to speak more quickly and to swallow the ends of sentences. If you are nervous during an interview, you may experience similar problems.

The first step you can take towards speaking more effectively is to control that nervousness. Breathe deeply and regularly before you begin. Pause when you are speaking to breathe deeply again. This will slow you down and help to keep any panic under control.

The next step is to examine some of the characteristics of effective speech and see if you can use them to improve your own performance.

Moderate the speed of your words During an interview, try to speak slightly more slowly than usual, particularly if you are speaking on a topic at some length. By slowing down, you will keep better control of what you are saying because you have time to think about the words you use. Be aware, though, that consistently slow speech can be very boring for the listener. There will be times when, quite naturally, you will speed up, such as when you react to a comment or answer an easy question.

Speaking slowly gives the person listening to you a chance to absorb and process what you are saying. An interviewer should be able to tell the difference between somebody who speaks slowly because they are considering

what to say and somebody who speaks slowly
to the point of being boring.

✎ Experiment with controlling the speed at
   which you speak. Read a newspaper
   article at your normal pace and tape the
   results. Now repeat the exercise but speed
   up. Record your voice reading the same
   article a third time, speaking more slowly
   than usual. It might sound a bit odd at
   first so keep practising. Concentrate on
   extending your control over the speed of
   your speech by varying the pace; read
   one sentence quickly, then slow down,
   then use your normal speed. What effect
   does this have on the way you interpret
   the words when you listen to the tape
   being played back?

Use pauses to break up your speech; they will
help you to group your thoughts and consider
your next sentence. In western societies, we
tend to be frightened of silence and rush on
regardless, filling any space in the conversation. When A stops talking, B immediately
starts. Eastern societies, particularly the Japanese and Koreans, see silence as a positive
aspect of dialogue, a sign of respect for the
other person. It is customary to pause before
the conversation continues to show that the
previous speaker's words have been listened to
and understood. Indeed, lengthy periods of
silence are considered by many Japanese to be
the most productive time spent in a meeting, a
time of mental summary when relevant facts
can be sorted out.

Project your words clearly. The volume at which you speak will be influenced by your surroundings. In an interview where you are sitting fairly close to just one other person, you can speak at normal conversational volume. If, during an interview, you have to make a presentation to a number of people sitting at the far end of the board room then speak up. Your aim is to make everything you say audible to every single person. They should be able to hear your words comfortably, without having to strain.

Embarrassment can make us speak more quietly; it is as if we do not want our words to be heard. Speaking more effectively does not, however, mean shouting. Keep your head up, breathe regularly and 'speak to the back of the room'. As voice coaches will tell you, when you project your words clearly, you push them out from the diaphragm, not from the back of the throat.

> *'Our meetings are chaired by the company secretary who knows everything about the business. The problem is that nobody can hear a word he says. He has a very quiet voice and tends to look down at the table when he is speaking. Somebody always asks him to speak up and for a couple of minutes he does, but then he tucks his chin down and becomes inaudible again. Continually asking him to speak up gets embarrassing, so after a couple of times we don't bother. No wonder we get through the agenda so quickly!'*

Vary the tone of your speech to add colour and emphasis to your words. By stressing particular words within a sentence, you can make a difference to the meaning of what you are saying.

✎ Try a simple exercise to see how this works. Speak the following phrase out loud placing the stress on a different word each time. How does the meaning of the sentence change?

He *went out with her.*
He **went** *out with her.*
He went **out** *with her.*
He went out **with** *her.*
He went out with **her.**

The pitch of your voice impacts on the listener. We generally find that a lower pitch is more attractive than a high pitched or piercing voice. What is the pitch of your voice – is it high or low? Tape yourself. Try raising and lowering the pitch and see how different it sounds.

Accents

The question of accents is an interesting one. Do accents influence people's perception of us? Some theorists believe that they do and the popular press has featured a number of stories about companies using staff with Newcastle accents because they sound more trustworthy and of the Prime Minister refining his accent into 'Estuary English' to make him more a man of the people. This is largely the product of stereotyping that would have us believe people with strong Yorkshire accents are the salt of the earth, Scouse accents denote 'scallies' and those who speak with an upper-class accent should always be listened to. One hopes that any interviewer would have the sense to ignore such myths.

What *is* important is clear enunciation of your words. The interviewer needs to be able to understand you. Strong dialect may prove a disadvantage but a regional accent should not.

TIPS FOR USING YOUR VOICE

- Use pauses for punctuation and give the other person a chance to absorb your words.

- Look at the person to whom you are speaking and maintain eye contact.

- Reinforce your words with nonverbal communication signals such as gestures with your hand, nodding, etc. But don't overdo these to the point where you become a human windmill or a John Cleese impersonator.

- Don't let your voice tail away at the end of a sentence. It makes it difficult for the listener to follow what you are saying. It can also make you sound ineffectual and unsure of yourself.

- Breathe! You may hold your breath when you are nervous; if you try this and speak at the same time, you will have problems. Take steady, regular breaths when you are listening to the other person to slow yourself down and pause for breath when you are speaking.

- Avoid verbal 'tics', those bad habits that are the spoken equivalent of biting your nails or pulling at your collar. Constant repetition of words and phrases such as *'OK'*, *'y'know'*, *'like'*, *'well'* and *'I mean'* can be a major irritant to the listener. They can also signal uncertainty and a lack of content in what you are saying.

- Relax. Nervousness is to be expected during the first few minutes of an interview but you have to let that nervousness go. If it continues throughout, then ask yourself why. What is it about this interview that makes you so afraid? Are you, perhaps, in a place that is not right for you?

Choose your words

GOLDEN RULE 11

Don't waffle.

Language can be very imprecise. Sometimes what the listener understands may not be precisely what you intended to convey, leading to confusion and a lack of clarity. Consequently, you must be careful with the words you use, particularly if you are talking about other people.

'He's relaxed in his approach' could mean *'he never gets flustered'* (positive) or *'he's careless'* (negative).

'She participates actively in the group' could

mean *'she makes a valuable contribution'* (positive) or *'she never shuts up and listens to anybody else'* (negative).

The rule is to be precise in what you say. Avoid euphemisms or smart remarks that can be misinterpreted. You may give out a very confused message if you use them.

Three hundred million people world wide use English as their first language but that does not mean all of those people use and understand words in the same way. Language is strongly influenced by culture. The greater the difference between the cultures from which people come, the greater the chance for cross-cultural miscommunication. The direct, up-front, straight talking communication we respect in Anglo societies is not the norm in every other country in the world. In many Arab, eastern and Latin American cultures, conversations take a far more circuitous route. Communication is implicit rather than explicit. Language is used to maintain harmony and the desire to maintain face (both one's own and others') rules out the direct 'no', replacing it with a more circumspect turn of phrase: *'I think much of what you are saying has value, however ...'*

In western cultures, being direct and 'cutting to the chase' is seen as a no nonsense, honest approach for busy people. This does not apply universally. Some cultures value circumlocution as a means of sounding out the other party in a conversation and of showing respect. It is important to understand that the preliminaries in an interview with Arab or Asian counterparts cannot be rushed;

they are as important as the rest of the conversation.

Jargon

You ask me what I do. Well, actually you know
I'm partly a liaison man and partly PRO
Essentially I integrate the current export drive
And basically I'm viable from ten o'clock till five.

John Betjeman, *The Executive*

Some people love jargon. Perhaps it makes them feel that they are part of an élite, a select club who speak their own language. For the rest of us, it can be profoundly irritating. Faced by somebody who continually uses terms or acronyms with which we are not familiar, we have the choice of pretending we understand (and running the risk of getting it wrong) or asking over and over again for words to be explained (which makes us feel foolish).

Your profession or specialism may well use particular terms as a form of shorthand. During an interview with somebody from the same discipline you can use these terms confidently, knowing that you will be understood. If you are talking to other people who may not share your experience, proceed with caution because your use of jargon could alienate them.

Equally annoying to some listeners are those overused metaphors that find their way into business environments: 'singing from the same hymn sheet', 'moving the goal posts' 'playing on a level playing field'. The first person who coined such phrases may have impressed their audience with their wit. When the phrases are used for the thousandth time, they lose their effectiveness and signal a lack of originality.

So keep your interpersonal dialogue with the CEO or the MD of the FMCG organisation that is extending an opportunity to you to discuss mutually profitable opportunities simple ...

....

LISTENING

GOLDEN RULE 12

If you don't listen, you don't know what is going on.

Listening involves more than simply hearing. When you listen you take in, process and respond to what you hear. In an interview, the ability to follow all three of these stages is very important. Short cutting, such as responding before you think about what you have heard, limits the effectiveness of your conversation.

> 'A lot of interviewees don't really listen to what you are saying. They are too busy leaping ahead and preparing their response to what you think you are going to say. Dialogue implies two-way communication and that means listening as well as talking.'

This is not an unusual complaint. Speaking well and communicating effectively through our words is a skill we are encouraged to practise. We pay less attention to our listening skills, not realising that unless we have the ability to listen well we cannot take full part in a dialogue.

There are a number of reasons why many of us find listening a difficult skill to master. External factors can make the process difficult. Noise is an ever present feature of our lives. We hear it but much of it does not directly affect us. We filter out unimportant noise; if we did not, we would experience sensory overload as our brains tried to cope with the thousands of messages it was asked to deal with. When you work in an open plan office you may hear the noise of other people coming and going, computer keyboards and telephones ringing, but these are background noises which you filter out and to which you pay little attention. The problem is that, having developed highly effective noise filters, we do not always switch these off when we should. We continue to filter out noise (such as the words somebody is speaking to us) that we need to listen to.

It is internal distractions, however, that are most likely to make us ineffective listeners. Our concern with our own thoughts can set up barriers which prevent us going through those three stages of hearing, processing and responding.

Let us consider these barriers in the context of an interview.

As you sit talking to the selector or your manager, what are you thinking about? Are you concentrating on their words or are you conducting your own 'stream of conscious-ness' monologue inside your head?

*'I know what she's going to ask me next but
I wonder if I should keep quiet about ... that
is a really ugly shirt she's wearing, I saw one
like it in ... God, it's hot in here ... I should
have told her about the time I ... I'm hungry
but I suppose we'll miss lunch ... I wonder if
the car's OK ...'*

The internal dialogue can be stimulated by
many factors including:

- something the other person has just said
- external factors such as physical
  discomfort or something you see or hear
- believing that you know what the other
  person is about to say
- boredom.

What results is a lack of concentration. Preoccupied with your own thoughts, you lose track
of what the interviewer is saying.

A second barrier to effective listening is a
fear, prevalent in the western world, of silence
which leads us to talk too much. A gap in
conversation is seen as an 'awkward pause'
that must immediately be filled. As we have
already seen, in many societies, silence is a
sign of respect and no conversation is without
its long, thoughtful pauses.

In an interview, you need to overcome these
barriers and become an effective listener so
that you increase your participation in the
dialogue and answer the interviewer's questions more appropriately.

Effective listening starts with increasing your
levels of concentration. You need to focus on
what is being said and shut out all extraneous
noise. At the same time, you must shut down

your internal dialogue. Don't attempt to predict what the next words will be or to start to prepare your own response. The only thing that matters is the words you are listening to and what they mean.

This is not a skill that you can expect to master immediately or to apply all the time. Such intense concentration can only be maintained for short periods but practising this skill will help. Try this:

✎ Video the television news. Twenty minutes later, watch the first three minutes of the broadcast. At the end of that period, switch off the television and write down as much as you can remember of what the newscaster said. You don't need to quote actual words but try to be as close as you can to what was said. Play back the tape and see how much of the news you listened to. Repeat the exercise, but increase the time from three to five minute excerpts.

Another tactic is keeping your mouth shut. As we have already said, many of us talk too much either because we fear silence or because we think we have so much of importance to say. The question is, of importance to whom? Are you talking because your words actively contribute to carrying the conversation forward? Or are you interrupting with an anecdote or statement that makes no real contribution but focuses attention back on you? Try this:

✎ Watch television (or listen to a play on the radio) and follow the dialogue.

Scripted dialogue cannot allow for too many interruptions because the flow of the drama would be lost, so characters tend to speak in whole sentences and complete what they want to say before the next person starts speaking. Now listen to a conversation – it could be on a train, at work or amongst your family members. Does the conversation follow the same pattern as the scripted dialogue? If not, can you identify the ways in which it differs?

As well as practising your skills so that you concentrate more fully, you also need to show the person you are talking to that you really are listening to them. You can do this through both verbal and nonverbal communication signals.

Verbal signals include:

- repeating or summarising what has been said to show that you have understood: *'So what you are saying is ...'*, *'If I've understood you correctly ...'*, *'Do you mean that ...'* (Don't go overboard on this because it can be profoundly irritating if somebody repeats *everything* you say to them)
- questions to clarify meaning
- continuity noises such as *'mm'*, *'ah ha'*, *'yes'*, etc.

Nonverbal signals include:

- facing the speaker
- maintaining eye contact and not letting your eyes wander around the room
- leaning forward to show that you are paying attention

- nodding to show that you are listening
- avoiding fidgeting, doodling, playing with your pen.

TIPS FOR EFFECTIVE LISTENING

- Focus on the speaker and try to shut out external distractions.
- Concentrate on what is being said not what you *think* is being said.
- Don't interrupt the other person – don't be afraid of silence.
- Show your attention by nodding and making sounds of encouragement.
- Use questions and summarise statements to make sure you have understood.

....

QUESTIONING TECHNIQUES

| GOLDEN RULE 13 |

If you understand basic questioning techniques, you have more control over a dialogue.

Questions form the basis of any interview but for questions to have any use, they must be effective. Effective questions have a clear purpose. They:

- gather knowledge and information
- draw out opinions
- keep a conversation focused and therefore relevant
- make the person you are talking to listen.

In conversation, we use a variety of questioning techniques to fulfil these objectives. Next time you talk to a colleague or a friend, listen to yourself. How do you elicit information from them? How do you find out what they are thinking? Can you see any pattern in the sort of questions you ask?

If you understand basic questioning techniques, it helps you to respond effectively during an interview and to give the interviewer the information they need. It also helps you avoid answering difficult questions badly. That, in turn, will boost your confidence and keep you calm.

How you answer questions when you are 'put on the spot' is largely dependent on your self-confidence. There may be times when you cannot answer or feel that you have been asked an unfair question. A confident job candidate or appraisee will stand their ground and politely but firmly state their case with a response such as, *'I don't think I'm in a position to answer that question'*, or *'I think that question is inappropriate'*. No, it's not easy to do this, but however uncomfortable you feel, it has to be better than saying something that you will later regret.

'When I was interviewed for my first teaching post, one of the panel asked me how I would persuade another member of staff to change their teaching style. It was a totally inappropriate question for someone at my level because I had no experience of managing staff. Luckily one of the other panel members vetoed the question and we moved on to other matters. Only afterwards did I find out that there was a battle going

*on within the faculty and a political point
was being made. I said I thought there was
no right answer and made a couple of points
that I thought might be relevant. Really, my
response to the question was immaterial.
They were fighting among themselves and
using me as ammunition.'*

Situations like this arise all the time. They will
never be easy to deal with and there is no
formula that helps you deal with them other
than to keep your nerve, say what you think
and refuse to be coerced into making inappropriate statements.

Questioning styles

*Effective management always means asking
the right questions.*

Robert Heller, *The Supermanagers*

To generate dialogue and gather information,
a good interviewer will rely heavily on open
and probing questions, occasionally use closed
and hypothetical questions, and avoid leading
and multiple questions. On the next few pages
you'll find out more about each of these types
of question together with tips on how to
answer them.

Open questions

In terms of the interview, this is the type of
question that should be used most frequently.
Open questions encourage you to 'open up',
to talk freely and give detailed answers. They

require minimum input from the interviewer but encourage you to give a lot of information.

Open questions frequently begin with:

- Who ... ?
- How ... ?
- Why ... ?
- When ... ?
- What ... ?
- Where ... ?

For example:

- *'What motivates you to do well?'*
- *'Why do you think we should employ you?'*
- *'How useful was your training in project management skills in helping you complete this job?'*

If you are asked an open question, the interviewer is expecting more than a one word answer. There is a line, however, between giving useful information in your reply and rambling on.

TIPS FOR ANSWERING OPEN QUESTIONS

- Keep to the point. If you are not absolutely sure what the interviewer wants to know, ask for clarification:
  - Interviewer: *'What has been your greatest achievement?'*
  - Interviewee: *'Do you mean during the last review period?'*

- Be concise. Don't waffle or ramble. One of the great dangers of the open question is that you, the interviewee, will talk too much. Present a relevant answer, stick to the point – and then stop.

- Be precise. If you have a particular point to make, try to use supporting evidence. If an interviewer asks you, *'Why do you want this job?'*, avoid a vague, *'Well, I thought I might enjoy it ...'* approach. Make your reasons clear and relate them to the employer's needs and understanding:
  - *'I'm looking for greater responsibility ...'*
  - *'I want to work for a bigger company ...'*
  - *'I have three years' experience of workng with products like yours ...'*
  - *'Your company has a reputation as the best in its field ...'*

Probing questions

The interviewer uses these questions to fill in the gaps behind your initial response. They are useful for examining an issue in greater depth. A sensitive, experienced interviewer will know how to use probing questions to elicit more information without being intrusive or making you feel threatened or uncomfortable.

Probing questions frequently relate to a point that has already been made and upon which you are asked to elaborate:

- *'You say you were unhappy with the final decision. Why was that?'*
- *'Why do you think that sequence of events happened?'*

TIPS FOR ANSWERING PROBING QUESTIONS

- Keep the interview on track by focusing on the question and responding directly to it. There is a danger with probing questions (particularly if you have established a good rapport with the interviewer) that you will say something that you later regret.

- Avoid being drawn into any discussion in which you comment on other people's personalities. An interviewer may ask probing questions about how you interact with colleagues. Keep your answers positive. Even if you thought your previous boss was totally incompetent, this is not the time or place to express your opinions.

- However much you might think a probing question is encouraging you to give your opinions on contentious issues such as race, gender, politics and religion, don't. Some interviewers may raise subjects like these to find out how you think or to see how easily you can be led into making indiscreet statements. Avoid the temptation to put the world to rights. The interview is not a platform for you to air your views.

Read the page at the end of this section on interview pitfalls.

Closed questions

Closed questions are used to elicit specific information. From the interviewer's point of view, this type of question can be used to confirm or clarify facts that demand a precise answer:

- Interviewer: *'Do you have a full driving licence?'*
  Interviewee: *'Yes.'*

- Interviewer: *'How long did you work in sales?'*
  Interviewee: *'Five years.'*

Closed questions are also useful for keeping the interview under control, particularly with a voluble or evasive interviewee.

This type of question can be useful up to a point, but too much reliance on closed questions prevents a real dialogue developing. The conversation can degenerate into a single question, single response session in which only a limited amount of information is exchanged and very little rapport is established. Closed questions also demand too much input from the interviewer. The basic principle during an interview is that you, the interviewee, should be doing 80 per cent of the talking and the interviewer should be *listening*.

TIPS FOR ANSWERING CLOSED QUESTIONS

- Be honest. Don't falsify your credentials, embroider your experience or make claims you cannot substantiate. The chances are that at some point your words will come back to haunt you.

- Watch the interviewer's nonverbal communication signals to see if they want more from you. An interviewer who relies heavily on closed questions may expect you to give additional information without further prompting. Raised eyebrows, nodding and silence can all indicate that you should give more detail.

Hypothetical questions

Hypothetical questions are used to put you in a situation and find out how you would respond. You may, for example, be given a scenario to interpret. This is useful for the interviewer to get some idea of how you think and to assess your personal skills. At the same time, the interviewer needs to remember that hypothetical questions get hypothetical answers and your answers may not necessarily reflect what you would actually do should that situation arise in real life.

Hypothetical questions may put you 'on the spot'. It can be unnerving if you are asked to give an opinion about something totally unfamiliar.

> *'I often use hypothetical questions as part of the interview. There are no right answers but they do help me assess how somebody's reasoning and thought processes work. I wouldn't expect the candidate to say anything for a few seconds. Hopefully they will analyse the question and think about their response before they start talking.'*

TIPS FOR ANSWERING HYPOTHETICAL QUESTIONS

- Think about your response before you give your answer. It is easy to jump in and fill the silence once the question has been asked only to find seconds later that you have misinterpreted.

- Clarify and break the question down if you need to:
  - Interviewer: *'If you are working with a project team and one of the members is proving very negative, what would you do?'*
  - Interviewee: *'Are we talking about a situation in which I manage the group, or am I a team member and somebody else is running the project?'*

- Don't pretend to know all the answers unless you really do. If the hypothetical question asks you to talk about a situation with which you are unfamiliar, then admit it. You may still be able to give a constructive response:
  - *'I'm not absolutely certain how I would react. I think the first thing I'd want to do is verify the facts and collect more information.'*

Leading questions

Leading questions suggest the answer to you. You are therefore tempted to give the response you believe the interviewer wants. Leading questions don't give the interviewer much information about you and they can lead you to make statements you don't really believe.

If the interviewer says, *'This job involves a lot of travel. I take it that won't worry you'*, you may be tempted to agree rather than raise any objections.

TIPS FOR ANSWERING LEADING QUESTIONS

- Don't feel that you have to agree. Some interviewers will use leading questions to test your strength of character and find out if you are willing to stand up for yourself.

- As with probing questions, beware of the question that leads you to comment on other people's shortcomings or on contentious issues.

- If you can't bring yourself to disagree openly, then stay neutral:
  - *'I really can't comment on that.'*

Multiple questions

A favourite with inexperienced or nervous interviewers who are having difficulty controlling their own thought processes, multiple questions can be confusing. Which part do you answer first? What does the interviewer really want to know? Where do you start – and where do you stop?

Multiple questions may give the interviewer a very limited amount of information since you will either answer the last part of the question first or focus on the part that is easiest to answer:

- *'So what about the work you've done with the complaints team? What was your particular function? Do you think the team as a whole is achieving an acceptable standard?'*

TIPS FOR ANSWERING MULTIPLE QUESTIONS

- Break the question down and answer each element if you can.

- Make it clear that is what you are doing. Ask the interviewer for guidance:
  - *'Which part of the question do you want me to answer first?'*

- Alternatively, you can repeat each element of the question before you answer it.

If the interviewer persists in asking multiple questions, use them to your advantage. Answer the parts of them with which you are most comfortable. If there is something the interviewer really needs to know they will repeat that element again. It may also encourage them to look at their own interviewing technique more closely!

The chart on the following pages summarises the main types of question you will come across. It shows their characteristics, the positive and negative features of the type of question and gives examples.

Frequently asked interview questions

Can you predict what questions you will be asked during an interview? To a degree. Organisations which recruit regularly and have invested time and money in training their interviewers will probably also have developed a systemised interview format in which certain questions will always be asked.

If you are really uncertain about how to address interview questions, then you may find some of the books available in high street bookstores will be useful. A number of writers have looked in detail at what these questions attempt to find out and how you can answer them.

Alternatively, you might like to try and develop answers for some of the most frequently asked questions which are listed on pages 155–157. These are not necessarily good questions – but they do come up a lot!

Question type	Characteristic	Example	Pros	Cons
Open	Need detailed answers	*'How did you benefit from the training?'*	Used to: • encourage dialogue • probe • invite lots of information • build rapport	• Can lead you to talk too much • Can lead to irrelevance • The conversation may become unstructured
Probing	Pick up on previous statements Need detailed answers	*'You say you want to work in London. Why is that?'*	Used to: • get in-depth information	• Can lead you to say too much • Can be used to introduce contentious issues • Conversation may move away from the job

Question type	Characteristic	Example	Pros	Cons
Closed	Invite one word answers – yes/no	*'Can you prepare this report?'*	Used to: • keep the conversation under control • bring the conversation back to the point • clarify information • check understanding	• Gain little new information • Don't encourage dialogue • Conversation can become 'interrogation'
Hypothetical	Invite a reaction to a given scenario or problem	*'What would you do if ... ?'*	Used to: • show how you approach a problem • assess your personal skills	• Can be unnerving • Answers may not really reflect what you would do

Question type	Characteristic	Example	Pros	Cons
Leading	Control direction of the conversation and suggest the required answer	*'This promotion is based in Kent. You won't mind relocating?'*	Used to: • help the interviewer exert control • test strength of character and your ability to stand up for yourself	• Your answers are directed • You may not say what you really think • Don't encourage dialogue
Multiple	Number of points raised at the same time	*'So what did you ...?* *Did it ...?* *Were you ...?'*	Used to: • confuse! • test your ability to handle more than one issue at a time	• You don't know what the interviewer really wants to know

Selection interviews

1. Why are you looking for a new job?

2. Why do you want to leave your present job?

3. What encouraged you to apply for this job?

4. What are you looking for in a new job?

5. What do you consider to be your greatest achievement in your last job?

6. Where do you see your career in three to five years' time?

7. Describe a task you have undertaken that illustrates your planning (communication, presentation, team management, etc.) skills.

8. What is the most difficult task you have faced in your work?

9. What do you know about the company?

10. Why do you want to work here?

11. How do you keep up with changes and developments in your field?

12. What did you enjoy most about your last job?

13. What did you enjoy least about your last job?

14. How would your current/most recent employer describe you?

15. What do you enjoy doing most at work?

16. What do you enjoy doing least at work?

17. Why should we offer you the job?

18. How do you cope with pressure?

19. How do you react to authority?

20. Tell me about yourself. (This is possibly one of the most annoying questions you could be asked and one of the hardest to answer. Ask the interviewer exactly what they want to know.)

Performance review questions

1. How do you think you have done since the last performance review meeting?

2. What did you find most satisfying about the work?

3. What did you find least satisfying about the work?

4. Why do you think the project went well?

5. Would you approach a similar task in a different way if it arose again?

6. How do you think we can best use your skills and abilities to address this issue?

7. Do you think you could take on more responsibility? If so, what would you like to do?

8. Do you feel that the objectives we agreed at the last interview were realistic?

9. What objectives would you like to agree for the next review period?

10. What resources do you need to achieve these objectives?

Development review questions

1. What other professional areas would you like to gain experience in?

2. What general direction do you feel your career is taking?

3. Where would you like your career to go?

4. Do you have any specific objectives for the next year?

5. What can we do to help you achieve those objectives?

6. What do you feel are your particular strengths?

7. What areas of your skills do you feel require further development?

8. Do you have any personal interests that would support your work?

9. Are there any training or development options you particularly want to follow?

10. How can you improve your contribution to the department?

TIPS FOR ANSWERING ALL INTERVIEW QUESTIONS

- Prepare before the interview so that you know what you are talking about.

- Answer honestly.

- Keep your answers straightforward.

- Ask for clarification if you are not sure what the interviewer wants to know. Ask directly or repeat and summarise the question.

- Take your time before you respond and think about the question.

- Be willing to answer all questions but don't be afraid to refuse if you think a question is inappropriate.

....

INTERVIEW PITFALLS

| GOLDEN RULE 14 |

Don't say anything you might regret later.

The section on leading and probing questions highlighted the dangers of saying too much during an interview. There is a further danger: that you may be asked questions that are discriminatory, too personal or in bad taste.

These questions may relate to your personal opinions or they may ask things about you that have no direct influence on your ability to do the job. Such questions may be asked because the interviewer wants to see how well you handle a difficult situation or simply because the interviewer is bad at their job and does not appreciate that he or she has crossed the line that defines a question as illegal.

I am free of all prejudice. I hate everyone equally.

W. C. Fields

There are certain areas of discussion that you should avoid:

- nationality, race, religion, sex or politics – if you have developed a rapport with the interviewer and feel at ease, it is easy to make an inappropriate comment and scarcely be aware of what you are saying. Pay attention to the general direction of the conversation and move it back to issues that are directly associated with the job

- your personal life – yes, some detail may be relevant, but beware of giving too much away. A potential employer does not need an in-depth analysis of your relationship with your partner, your parents or your friends

- personalities – if you are asked, *'What did you think of your last boss?'* avoid the temptation to make negative comments. You will have to work with a lot of different people during your career, some of whom you will like and some of whom you may loathe. Showing a lack of respect or negativity about other people reflects badly on you and could influence an interviewer's decision about your ability to fit into their organisation.

Discrimination against another person on the grounds of their gender or race is unlawful. The Sex Discrimination Act 1975 states that no person should be treated less favourably than another because of their sex or marital status. Under the provisions of the Act, it is unlawful to discriminate:

- in arrangements made for determining who should be offered employment
- in terms and conditions of employment
- in refusing or deliberately omitting to offer employment on the grounds of sex
- in preventing access to promotion, training, transfer or any other benefits, facilities or services.

Discrimination is allowed where a person's sex is a genuine occupational qualification. For example, a job may have to be offered to a man or woman to preserve the decency and privacy of their clients.

The Race Relations Act of 1976 says that individuals should not be discriminated against because of their race, colour, ethnic or national origin and makes provisions about what is unlawful. In Northern Ireland discrimination on the grounds of religious belief or political opinion is also unlawful.

The law specifies two types of discrimination:

- **direct discrimination** is easier to identify. It occurs when applicants are clearly disadvantaged by their sex, race or religion – for example if application forms are not sent to applicants from ethnic minorities

- **indirect discrimination** is more difficult to identify. It occurs when an organisation imposes a condition that only a certain group of people can satisfy – and that condition is not justified in terms of the job. For example, if a sales organisation believed that young women would boost its sales performance and didn't seriously consider applications from men or women over 40, it would be guilty of indirect discrimination.

Indirect discrimination may include making assumptions about how someone will fulfil a job because of their sex, race or religion, for example:

- asking a woman about her plans for having a family but not asking men about their plans
- asking an applicant how they would deal with colleagues of a different race.

Age discrimination

At present, there is no legislation which makes it unlawful to discriminate against a candidate on the grounds of their age. There is evidence that such discrimination does exist, although researchers argue as to how extensive the problem really is. Some practices, such as refusing to employ women of childbearing age in case they suddenly go off on maternity leave, could be classed as indirect discrimination under the existing legislation of the Sex Discrimination Act.

The government has, on occasion, highlighted the problem of employers discriminating against job applicants on the grounds of their age and, at the time of writing, is putting forward suggestions to encourage a more open attitude towards more mature candidates.

Employers should be more concerned about your ability to do the job than your age. Mature candidates can help themselves by being clear about their skills and experience and presenting these succinctly and effectively. Another concern which may lead employers to favour younger candidates (besides being able to pay them less!) is the belief that they will be more up to date in both their knowledge of technology and management techniques. Age is no barrier to keeping abreast of developments in your career area; make sure interviewers are aware of any recent training you have taken and show them how you keep up with changes in your profession.

Companies which do favour younger recruits will usually make this clear very early in the recruitment procedure either by setting target ages for applicants or by pre-selecting and turning down applicants over a certain age. If reference *is* made to your age during an interview, highlight the experience your many years in employment have given you.

TIPS FOR HANDLING INTERVIEW PITFALLS

- Stay calm and don't give an immediate answer.

- Ask for clarification. If the question borders on the illegal then this may show the interviewer that you are aware of what they are doing.

- Have the confidence to refuse to answer. State firmly, *'I don't think that question is relevant to my ability to do this job.'*

If the interview has degenerated to a level where you are being asked questions that are openly discriminatory or distasteful, you may be tempted to stop the proceedings and march out of the room. It would be more effective to refuse to give a direct answer and make a careful note of what is being said by the interviewer. Afterwards, you may wish to seek professional advice not only to redress the difficulties that have arisen in your situation but to prevent the employer playing the same game with other candidates. Contact your local Citizen's Advice Bureau to find the name of a specialist in employment law. Alternatively, if you are a member of a trade union, it may be able to offer advice.

....

RECEIVING FEEDBACK

So far, Part Three of *Interviews and Appraisals* has looked at the skills you need (and can improve on) to perform well during a selection or appraisal interview.

The final section deals with receiving and understanding feedback. The circumstances it describes are very different. Feedback from a selection interview comes after the event and at your instigation. You have a choice whether you contact the selector and ask them to discuss the job market, your application techniques and interview performance in the hope that you will receive useful advice that you can use in future job applications.

During performance and development review interviews, feedback is an integral part of the proceedings. It tells you what your employer thinks of the way in which you are working and what direction your career is taking.

Being able to receive feedback and profit from it is an important skill. Feedback is not criticism, although many of us are too quick to see it that way. It is an important part of any dialogue. It helps you to understand how other people respond to your actions and how you affect them. Used constructively, feedback can help you to improve your performance and to find new and more effective ways of working.

Feedback after selection interviews

GOLDEN RULE 15

Feedback after selection interviews will help you perform better in future job applications.

What happens after a selection interview if you don't get the job? For many of us there is a sense of personal rejection, a tendency to think 'I wasn't good enough'. Alternatively, we may look for tenuous excuses for our lack of success: 'They already knew who they wanted and the whole interview process was really a sham.' This is speculation. Unless you are willing to continue your dialogue with the selector, you don't know why another person was offered the job.

Surprisingly few job seekers ask selectors for feedback. They prefer to forget that particular interview and move on to the next application rather than return to the selector to discuss what happened. It is an understandable reaction but it excludes the possibility of getting profitable advice which can help them refine their application and interview techniques for the future.

Some employers will not be willing to give feedback and the polite, 'We thank you for your interest but regret to inform you that on this occasion your application was unsuccessful ...' letter is the most you will get. Many other employers will be prepared to spend time talking to you either in person or on the telephone to discuss the selection process and your application.

You can use the information from these discussions (the feedback) to assess and improve:

- your chances of finding the job you want
- your knowledge of the employment area you have chosen
- your CV and application form
- your interview technique.

  'If somebody has taken the trouble to go through the whole rigmarole of applying for a job, the least I can do is to spend half an hour talking to them if they are not successful. Not many of them ask me, though.'

Making the approach

Once you have received the selector's decision about your application, wait three or four days then telephone and ask if you can arrange a meeting to gather feedback. Ideally, you want a short face-to-face meeting. If that is not possible, ask for a convenient time when you can call back to discuss the matter over the phone.

The way in which you make this first approach is very important. Make it clear from the outset that you are not getting in touch to demand an explanation of why you didn't get the job. No employer is going to find time to talk to you if they fear they will face a barrage of criticism.

Be precise and positive about your reasons for calling and identify the questions you want to discuss *before* you phone. You may want to discuss:

- employment prospects in your particular field
- other opportunities within the organisation
- ways in which you can improve your profile through additional training and development
- areas of your experience that can be extended to make you a more suitable candidate.

This gives the person with whom you are talking something on which to focus. It also puts the discussion onto a neutral footing and suggests that you are not taking the rejection personally and seeking vengeance!

During the meeting

Having identified the questions you want to ask, use them when you meet the selector. Listen to the replies; you could gather a lot of useful information. For example, if the selector tells you that more than 150 people applied for this post, you may want to find out why this is such a competitive field. What was the calibre of other applicants? What particular factors influenced the employer in creating a short list and sifting through the applicants at interview? If this area of employment is so competitive, should you be looking at related functions and, if so, which? What advice can the selector offer?

Look for inside information on the particular market sector in which you want to work. What is the general direction for careers in this field? Is it a growth area or one in which opportunities are declining? Would your prospects of getting the job you want increase if you looked in a different region of the country? Should you be widening the net and targeting more diverse types of employer – and, if so, how?

You may receive more information than you anticipated, such as details of companies which are expanding and recruiting and names of contacts within human resource departments.

Ask about training and development opportunities that might benefit your job search. Should you be thinking about taking additional training courses? Is there any particular skills area that would help you? What new technology should you be aware of and proficient in?

The selector may be able to give you useful suggestions about how to extend your experience within your current job to increase your effectiveness, such as secondments to other functions, job rotation, placements and work shadowing. All of these can offer valuable new insights and skills.

Don't be afraid to ask for advice about the way in which you tackled the application procedure for the job you didn't get but, again, be precise about what you want to know.

- *'Are there any areas of my CV that need to be strengthened?'*
- *'As an employer, what personal skills do you look for in a candidate for this type of job?'*

The advice you receive will be worth listening to because it comes from the people you most want to impress – those who carry out the interviews and select the staff.

TIPS FOR RECEIVING FEEDBACK AFTER A
SELECTION INTERVIEW

- Decide before the meeting what information would be most useful to you.

- Make a list of the questions you want to ask.

- Determine how long the meeting will last and don't stay any longer.

- Ask precise, fact-based questions.

- Remain objective and distance yourself from any disappointment you feel about not getting this job.

- Don't use the feedback meeting to justify yourself or argue why you should have got the job.

- Listen to what the selector has to say.

- Don't interrupt or become preoccupied by the points *you* want to make.

- Watch yourself and the selector and note signals that mean the meeting is drawing to a close. If you find yourself wanting to argue, or the person to whom you are talking starts to look distracted, then it is time to leave.

Finally, thank the selector for their time and assistance. They have taken the trouble to talk to you and try to help. Recognise their effort. It will help you to leave a lasting and positive impression and you never know when another suitable vacancy might arise with this company.

Feedback during appraisal interviews

Feedback during appraisal interviews is intended to help you.

Part of the appraisal interview, whether it is a performance or development review, consists of receiving feedback about your performance and your potential for development. Experienced managers will be trained to deliver feedback in such a way that you do not feel threatened by what they say. Ideally you should both leave the meeting with a sense that something constructive has been achieved.

To benefit from the feedback you receive in an appraisal interview, you need to use all your communication skills. You will find it useful to look at the sections in this book on effective listening, speaking and nonverbal communication.

Many employees make the mistake of thinking that they have a limited role to play in the appraisal interview and that they are there to receive an opinion rather than to contribute However, there are many ways in which *you* can make the whole feedback process easier and more productive.

1. **Remain focused.** Remember that the purpose of the interview is to help you to do your best for yourself, your team and your organisation.

2. **Discuss specifics.** Generalised statements of praise from your manager may boost your ego but do little to help you improve your style of work. Ask *why* your performance in a particular area was good. Ask your manager to pinpoint the actions you have taken that have helped your team or department. Similarly, ask your manager to be precise about particular areas that need improvement.

3. **Look for answers.** If problems have arisen during the review period, how can these be addressed? Constructive suggestions from both you and your manager are needed rather than continually going over why a problem arose.

4. **Ask questions.** The appraisal interview is a time for an exchange of information and ideas, not a time when you are judged and given a verdict. Use the opportunity, particularly during a development review, to discuss your future with the organisation. Ask your manager:

- *'How do you see my career progressing during the next twelve months?'*
- *'How can I increase my contribution to the team / department / company?'*
- *'What action can I take to bring about that progress?'*

5. **Be willing to listen**. Even if your manager doesn't always tell you what you want to hear, you need to listen. Avoid jumping to conclusions or thinking 'what's the point?' if the discussions don't go the way you anticipate.

6. **Negotiate**. When it comes to setting new objectives, be prepared to negotiate targets that are acceptable to both of you. Don't say yes to everything because you feel you have no choice. The result will be targets you cannot meet, causing you frustration at a later stage. Read the section about setting objectives when you are preparing for interview on pages 78–80.

7. **Clarify and finalise**. Make sure that you are clear about what is agreed. Again, this means focusing on detail, repeating statements and being definite about what is expected of you. Find out when you will get a written report of the meeting that sets out your new objectives.

8. **Use the feedback**. It should be the basis of your action plan for the future. From your discussions with your manager you should be able to draw a number of conclusions:

- I have performed well in these areas, therefore I can go on to ...
- I could improve in these areas. I will do this by ...

One aspect of feedback that merits more detailed examination is how you deal with negative feedback if a situation arises when your manager needs to discuss aspects of your performance that you need to change and improve.

Negative feedback

| GOLDEN RULE 17 |

Don't overreact to negative feedback.

During a performance review interview you will discuss your performance and what you have achieved during the last review period. Much of what you hear will (hopefully) be positive. Managers generally understand the importance of praising past achievement and using it as a motivator for future performance. It may be necessary, however, to talk to you about areas in which you have not carried out your work to the desired standard or to discuss ways in which your work-related behaviour needs to be modified. In business parlance, this is known as delivering negative feedback. You may well have your own way of describing it.

> *'Performance review is fine when your manager tells you what you want to hear – that you are doing well and they have great hopes for your future. When they are critical, though, however much you know the criticism is justified, it is hard to stay objective and not feel threatened.'*

A manager may draw attention to unsatisfactory aspects of performance in order to prevent a situation from deteriorating still further. It could be that you are unaware of the problem and without advice will not see the need to change. It could be that you have unrealistic ideas about your own performance or capabilities. Unless the problem is dealt with promptly, you could be on the way to more major problems, leading to confrontations in the future. By listening and accepting the negative feedback now, you are being given the chance to change.

Dealing with negative feedback is very, very difficult for all the parties involved. Many managers will avoid discussing problems rather than risk appearing critical. Others, embarrassed by the task they face, communicate ineffectively thus damaging relationships and not achieving the results they seek.

At the same time, it demands tremendous effort and maturity on the part of the person receiving the feedback, together with an ability to distance emotions from the problems that are being discussed, for negative feedback to produce a positive result.

Good interviewers are trained to deliver negative feedback in a direct, constructive manner. The golden rule for interviewers is to focus on the problem or aspect of behaviour that needs to be improved rather than on personal characteristics. They should look at ways in which performance can be improved, not the individual's personality.

You, as the person receiving the negative feedback, must accept that the comments your manager makes are not a slight on your character. They are constructive suggestions that will help you work more effectively and achieve more. They are being made to help you; you are not being criticised.

This is easy to say, but often difficult to do. Most of us find it hard not to bridle when shortcomings in our performance are brought to our attention. It is a reflex action to say, *'Yes, but –'*, or *'It wasn't my fault –'* We have been avoiding negative feedback since we were children so why should it become acceptable now?

Nevertheless, receiving negative feedback is part of your job. Your manager has a responsibility to help you perform to the best of your ability, so that you – and the organisation – can achieve optimum productivity. So it is time to put aside the ploys of childhood, to stop taking negative feedback as a personal insult and to learn to listen and use it to your advantage.

This is where your ability to remain calm, dispassionate and objective about work is so important. If that seems impossible because you still can't bear receiving criticism, then you will have to use all your powers of self-discipline to:

- listen to what is being said
- ask for advice on how you can improve
- avoid retorting *'But ...'*
- ask for more information
- avoid passing the blame onto somebody else or some fault in the system
- stay relaxed.

Listen to what is being said

Focus on what the manager is saying about your performance. Try to shut out all the small voices in your head that drown out their words. You have already looked at some barriers to effective listening so you will be aware that one of the worst culprits is focusing on your internal dialogue rather than the person who is speaking to you.

Break down what is being said. A good manager will talk about something in your behaviour that you can change and will give you constructive advice. For example, if you are receiving negative feedback about your ability to meet deadlines don't, in your own mind, translate this into a general criticism of your character: 'She's implying that I'm bad at meeting deadlines because she thinks I'm either disorganised or lazy.'

Look at the particular episode when your work was late and identify:

- why you missed the deadline
- how you reacted when you knew your work would be late
- what external factors were involved
- how you could have limited the effect of these external factors
- how you would react if a similar situation occurs again.

Ask for advice

A good manager will offer you support to overcome work-related difficulties and any negative feedback will be accompanied by constructive advice. This may take the form of reorganising your workload, or offering additional training and support. Take these suggestions in the spirit in which they are given rather than rejecting them. They could help you to improve and thus remove the problem. If advice from your manager is not immediately forthcoming, then ask for it. Acknowledge that there is a problem and ask how your manager thinks you should deal with it.

Avoid immediate retorts

Even if you think the negative feedback about

your performance is unjustified, hold your tongue. An immediate reaction in the form of a defensive remark will achieve nothing. What you will do is start a spiral which defeats real communication:

- you feel under attack – *'She's not being fair.'*
- you respond defensively – *'That's just not true!'*
- your manager feels under attack – *'He thinks I'm getting at him.'*
- your manager responds defensively – *'Oh yes, it is!'*

Sarcasm is another form of defensiveness. It might make you feel better at the time to show just how sharp you can be and to 'get one over' with a smart remark, but what do you actually achieve? You have not addressed the problem, your manager becomes wary of you and constructive communication is blocked.

If you feel that you *are* being criticised unfairly, wait a couple of days before you present your own case. This gives you time to collect any evidence you need to support your position. You may also find that matters that seemed terribly important during the review meeting are less so when you consider them more calmly away from the interview room. Save your energy for dealing with issues that are really important.

Ask for more information

Instinctively when we are faced with negative feedback, we want to get the whole conversation finished. It may seem odd to suggest that you should ask for more detail about ways in which you have not met the expectations of your manager but the more knowledge you have, the more able you will be to address problems or to deal with negative feedback that is unjustified.

Keep your immediate reactions under control until your manager has finished summarising their viewpoint. If you feel that the negative feedback is not justified, then ask for more information. You cannot respond adequately unless you know exactly what the problem is. Ask for specific examples of ways in which your manager thinks you need to improve.

Negative feedback such as: *'You occasionally have difficulty in communicating your intentions to the rest of the team'* mean very little. You want to know about specific occasions when you did this so that you understand exactly what incidents the feedback relates to.

As we have already said, if you feel that negative feedback about your performance is unfair, then collect evidence to support your viewpoint and to show why this negative feedback is inaccurate. This may involve collecting information or discussing the matter with other colleagues. Be cautious; you are not asking them to take sides but simply asking for their perspective on a particular issue. Then wait a couple of days. If you still feel strongly that you need to discuss the matter further, request another meeting with your manager and present your case.

Avoid passing the blame

If a criticism is unjustified, then you will be able to show your manager that they have not fully understood the situation. For example, if you missed a number of deadlines because information you needed from another sector of the company did not arrive on time, then you should be able to prove this. It is up to both of you to look for a way to improve the communication system between departments to stop the problem recurring.

Highlighting a problem that arises because of colleagues or 'the system' is different from passing the blame. It involves acknowledging the problem exists and looking for positive action to alleviate it. Saying *'Well, it's not my fault. I can't rely on* x *to supply the goods'*, does nothing to improve your situation. *'There is a problem with getting the information through on time and I think we need to liaise more closely and develop a new reporting system with* x*'*, does.

Stay relaxed

Yes, it is easier said than done, but what good will it do you to get upset? Are you going to achieve more by becoming aggressive or tense?

Your manager may find delivering negative feedback a difficult task. It has to be done, but they may not like it any more than you do. So use your communication skills to keep the meeting focused and defuse any tension.

You can achieve this by indicating that you understand your manager's point of view and that you acknowledge elements of the feedback. This does not necessarily mean that you accept everything that is said by them but you recognise that difficulties exist and need to be resolved. An acknowledgement can do much to reduce the stress on both sides: *'I appreciate that my performance in this area hasn't been as effective as we anticipated. What do you suggest we do?'*

Note the use of *'we'*. You are emphasising your commitment to the team and to the organisation. You are recognising that you all have to work together. You are implying that you did not achieve the target that you both set, therefore you both need to work on the problem. You have moved the focus of the conversation away from yourself and firmly onto the problem. A good manager will follow your lead and work with you towards constructive remedies.

'I had no idea how difficult it is to talk to staff about their performance until I had to do it. You are walking through a minefield of other people's sensitivities, pride and ego and you know that however much praise you give, it is the single criticism you make that they will remember.'

TIPS FOR RECEIVING NEGATIVE FEEDBACK

- Remain calm.
- Retain your self-control.
- Focus on the problem and don't get personal.
- Acknowledge comments and ask for more information or specific examples of ways in which you have not performed to the expected standard.
- Don't react defensively, avoid sarcasm or sharp remarks.
- Listen to what is being said.
- Ask for advice.
- Be willing to take advice.

What you don't have to do is accept unfounded criticism, personal comments or judgements on your character. Your manager has no right to chastise or patronise you. If you feel this is happening, then make it clear that you feel the conversation is unproductive and you would like to resume it at a later date. If your manager refuses, or continues to use tactics that you feel are unfair, it may be necessary to ask for the services of an intermediary who will sit in and monitor the interview.

....

MONITORING YOUR PROGRESS

There is a temptation to see any interview as an end in itself but interviews are only part of the selection or appraisal processes. To ensure that your job search or your general progress at work is producing results, you need constantly to monitor and review your actions in the light of what the interview has taught you.

The easiest way to make this monitoring process work efficiently is to write things down. A useful tool for both job seekers and those in employment is the personal log book.

After a selection interview

GOLDEN RULE 18

Keep records of your job applications and interviews.

Applying for a job is a lengthy process that

demands a lot of effort. (For more detail see *Job Seeking*, also in the *Career PowerTools* series.) First you have to find an appropriate vacancy. Then you need to prepare your CV or complete an application form and send this to the prospective employer. If you are successful in getting through the pre-selection stage and the employer thinks you may be suitable for the position, you will be invited for interview or to an assessment centre, or both. Then there is the period of waiting until the employer makes a decision and lets you know whether or not you have got the job.

The tension that this process can generate should not be underestimated. For most of us, searching for the right job is a period of intense emotional highs and lows. There is excitement when you source a vacancy that you like the look of, impatience as you wait for decisions, nervousness before an interview, euphoria if you are offered the job and disappointment if you are not. Small wonder that many job seekers apply for one job at a time, and if they are unsuccessful, wait some time before they feel confident enough to go through the process again.

If you are seriously looking for a new job, you will not have time to lick your wounds each time you receive a letter of rejection. For job seeking to be successful, it must be a systematic process that you approach in the same way you would approach a task at work. You must keep up the impetus and never stop searching for vacancies and submitting applications. You must anticipate that, until you find the job you want, the search will take over a large part of your life.

One way that you can stay on track is to

monitor your job search and keep a log book to show your progress. This need not be a complex document or a particularly time-consuming exercise, but it should be detailed enough to help you focus on the aspects of your search that are going well and those that need improvement.

Keeping records

Set up a diary sheet to record every job-seeking activity you complete. This should include a list of the approaches you make, the interviews you attend and the feedback meetings you set up. You could use a system as simple as the one shown below.

Vacancy			
CV/application form			
Reply received			
Interview			
Outcome			
Feedback meeting			

In the vacancy column, write the date and how you found out about the vacancy; this could be through an advertisement, speculative letter, a network contact or a recruitment agency. In the remaining columns, write the dates you send in your CV or application form (and the closing date for applications, if there is one), receive an acknowledgement, are asked for interview, receive the employer's decision and take part in a feedback meeting.

Keeping a log like this will help you maintain the momentum of your job search. Unless you work in a very specialised area where vacancies are few and far between, you should be aiming to make at least two contacts a week to potential employers. With so many applications pending, it is easy to forget where you stand with each prospective employer. The log will also give you a psychological boost if you reach a point when you feel that your job search is not progressing well. Here you have a written record of the work you are putting in, work that will eventually produce results.

A log book or diary helps you monitor the selector's actions. If you have not received a reply to your application within ten days of the closing date for recruitment, call up the organisation. Tell them that you are checking to ensure your application was received and find out what time frame the employer is working to. You should be able to discover when pre-selection will be completed and when short listed candidates will be called for interview.

You might find it useful to add an assessment of any interviews you attend to your notes. Take a little time to review your performance. What went well? Where did you feel you could improve? Were there any aspects of the interview that were unfamiliar to you? Were there questions that you found difficult to answer? If so, how would you approach these if they came up again? A brief analysis of your experiences in the interview room can help you to prepare for your next meeting with a selector.

Monitoring progress after an appraisal interview

GOLDEN RULE 19

Keep a record of your daily progress at work.

The annual appraisal interview is over. You breathe a sigh of relief that you survived it once again, then forget about the whole appraisal process until you get a letter twelve months later telling you the date of the next interview. Meanwhile, your manager fills in the forms, sends them back to the human resources department, grateful that a difficult part of their job is over for another year. They also forget about appraisal until the last minute scramble to collect information a couple of days before the next round of interviews start.

Unfortunately, for far too many people this is exactly what happens. Appraisal is seen as the interview itself, a one-off event that has nothing to do with day-to-day routine. Once the interview and paperwork are complete, the appraisal process is forgotten.

Such an attitude undermines the purpose of the appraisal system, which is to encourage continual improvement in the workplace. It is easy to see why it happens, though. If ongoing appraisal takes place, the degree of monitoring and documentation required to continually evaluate progress could become so time-consuming that it would leave no scope for you – or your manager – to do anything else.

Some organisations have systems in place to monitor progress throughout the review period. This may involve weekly or fortnightly informal meetings with a team or with management to discuss progress and iron out minor problems. Managers will use these meetings to collect information throughout the whole review period. Staff may also contribute to this ongoing process by filling in a log book to monitor their own performance.

It is in your interests to monitor your own progress after the appraisal interview so that you have clear evidence of how well you perform in your job and a record of any problems you encounter. This evidence is important; you can use it during the next performance review interview. Why rely on your manager to collect all the necessary information? You do the job, so you have a better idea of what goes on in your part of the workplace. Start monitoring your progress yourself.

If your organisation has an 'open' appraisal system, you should receive a copy of your manager's comments after the interview. You will also have a list of the objectives that you both agreed for the next review period. It is these that you can use as the basis of your own monitoring process. Keep this list of objectives to hand and start up a file to accompany them.

1. **Keep your monitoring system simple**. Six months or a year is a long time to remember everything that happens at work, so

start a log book. Use a desk diary specifically for this purpose or make notes in a loose leaf folder. Note any key achievements and any problems, however minor, that cause you difficulties. You do not need to make detailed notes, but to compile an aide memoire. Use the log book to note any thoughts about your work that might be relevant to your review.

2. **Keep checking your progress**. If a problem persists and is preventing you achieving any of your specified objectives, then look back over your log book. When and how did the problem start? Has it persisted for more than a month? If so, you may want to consult your manager and bring the situation to their attention. Do not wait until the next formal appraisal interview to raise the issue.

3. **Be realistic about your objectives**. If you are struggling to achieve some of your objectives, look at them again. Did you and your manager set over-ambitious targets? Why do you now think they were over-ambitious? Conversely, if you find yourself achieving your objectives too easily then you are not stretching yourself. Are you satisfied with work that offers no real challenge? Easily achieved objectives provide little stimulation.

4. **Give yourself time**. Give your manager time, too. The objectives you set during your formal appraisal interview will not be achieved overnight. For example, if during a development review interview, you both agree that you need further training in a specific area, then make sure that training materialises. Bear in mind, however, that it may take some

weeks for your manager to get the necessary approvals and to find a suitable course. Don't forget about your objective but balance your enthusiasm against practicalities. It can take time for new ideas to get off the ground.

5. **Note any changes in your situation**. Keep a careful eye on what your job actually involves. If your job description changes during the review period, write down what new responsibilities you have had to take on, even if these are only for a temporary period. By the time your review comes around you may already be taking additional responsibilities for granted but in the initial stages they can take up a lot of time and energy and contribute to you not achieving your objectives. Look what happened to this employee:

'At my appraisal interview, my line manager (who doesn't work in this branch) and I set a number of objectives, one of which was to develop a new marketing initiative to bring in more first time buyers to our branch. Unfortunately during the next six months we were plagued by staffing problems and I was continually covering for other members of staff, which left me no time to do anything but the basics of my own job. Gradually the situation resolved itself. Another six months later, when the next formal review came round, I still hadn't made much progress on the marketing work. All I could do was try to explain how hard the staff shortages had affected me, but it sounded rather lame.'

6. **Look for new opportunities**. What would make your job more rewarding and interesting? What development opportunities have

you become aware of during the course of the year? Make a note of them in your log book. Get used to identifying opportunities for yourself rather than waiting for them to be suggested by somebody else and present them to your manager at your next review.

Keeping your own records can go a long way towards helping you create the sort of job you want. It makes you a far more active participant in the appraisal process. Use the notes you have made throughout the review period to put together an outline of what *you* have achieved, how *you* think things can be improved and what *you* want to see happen next.

....

AND FINALLY ...

Monitoring your progress brings you to the end of *Interviews and Appraisals* and to the last of the Golden Rules:

GOLDEN RULE 20

Keep working to improve your interview technique.

The way you perform during an interview is influenced by many different factors, the most important of which are your communication skills and your confidence. One impacts on the other. If you feel that you communicate well, relate positively to other people regardless of their job and have few problems in getting your opinions across, then you will not find interviews intimidating. You will approach interviews with confidence.

Practise your communication skills all the time and consciously use them to improve your interview technique.

TIPS FOR IMPROVING YOUR INTERVIEW PERFORMANCE

- Take responsibility for your part in the interview.
- Recognise the importance of thorough preparation.
- Monitor your performance during interviews.
- Think about your communication skills. Identify your strengths and build on them.
- Identify your weaknesses and continually work to eradicate them.

CONCLUSION

The section on monitoring your progress after selection and appraisal interviews brings you to the end of *Interviews and Appraisals*. Hopefully you will have found some of the advice useful and this book will have stimulated you to look closely at your own approach to interviews and think about ways in which you can improve your technique.

THE GOLDEN
RULES

As you read through the various sections of Interviews and Appraisals, you encountered the Golden Rules. Here is a recap of the points they made. Remember, these are simple, sensible guidelines that you can apply to almost any interview situation.

Rule 1.
You cannot expect to perform well in an interview unless you are adequately prepared.

Interviews are important events in your professional life. If you invest some time in thinking about and preparing for the interview, you will be better equipped to present your case and to meet the interviewer with confidence.

Rule 2.
Research the organisation, the job and your ability to fulfil its requirements *before* the selection interview.

Show your enthusiasm by finding out all you can about the company you want to join and the job for which you are applying. Information is readily available through companies themselves, libraries and the Internet. Before the interview plan how you can show the interviewer that you possess the skills, experience and personal qualities that make you the most suitable applicant for the job.

Rule 3.
Many selectors ask similar questions so you can think about your responses before the interview.

Selectors have to be thorough in order to find the right person for the job. Some of the questions they ask will be detailed, probing and difficult to answer if you haven't given them some thought beforehand. Look at lists of frequently asked questions and think about how you would approach them and always look for evidence to support any claims you make.

Rule 4.
Leave nothing to chance and check the details of your interview.

Arriving late, going to the wrong office (or, as one job candidate did, the wrong branch in the wrong town!) will throw you completely off balance. Make sure you know where you are supposed to be and when and give yourself plenty of time to get there.

Rule 5.
Appraisal is a two-way process that demands input from you as well as from your manager.

An appraisal interview is not a session in which you are tried, judged and found wanting. It is a process designed to help you, your manager and the organisation you work for. None of which can be achieved unless you are willing to play your part in the proceedings and help your appraiser to evaluate your performance and potential.

Rule 6.
Contribute to your appraisal interview by setting your own objectives.

Identify what you want out of your job and go into your appraisal interview prepared to ask for it. Set your own objectives, making sure they focus on areas that are important to you and that they are SMART.

Rule 7.
Your appearance tells the interviewer a lot about you.

First impressions count for a great deal in any situation and interviews are no exception. Like it or not, interviewers make judgements based on how you look, so it pays to invest a little time and money in creating a professional image.

Rule 8.
If you care about yourself, you will care about the business.

Casual, windswept and unkempt may be your personal style, but it raises the question that you may take the same approach to your work. Looking good means paying attention to your personal grooming as well as the clothes you wear.

Rule 9.
Everything you say can be reinforced or undermined by your nonverbal communication signals.

Everyone gives messages all the time through their posture, gestures, eye contact, tone of voice and other nonverbal communication signals. The messages you send should complement your words. It is no good saying all the right things during an interview if you sound and look bored and miserable; it is these negative signals the interviewer will almost certainly home in on.

Rule 10.
Use your voice as well as your words to engage and keep the interviewer's attention.

Your voice is a powerful tool so learn to use it to your advantage. Varied pitch and emphasis all serve to make you sound more interesting and to help the listener focus on your words. A monotonous drone could put your interviewer to sleep.

Rule 11.
Don't waffle.

Say what you want to say clearly and precisely, avoiding pretentious phrases or unnecessary jargon. Then shut up.

Rule 12.
If you don't listen, you don't know what is going on.

Listening skills are important. Learn to go beyond hearing the words to actually listening to what is being said. Concentrate on the speaker, don't interrupt and think about what their words really mean rather than jumping in with a quick remark half way through.

Rule 13.
If you understand basic questioning techniques, you have more control over a dialogue.

A good interviewer will use a variety of different styles of questions to elicit information from you. By understanding what those styles are and how interviewers use them, you are more likely to give them the answers they are seeking.

Rule 14.
Don't say anything you might regret later.

Be wary of making any statement that could be used against you. In particular, avoid commenting negatively about your colleagues or your current boss. Religion, sex, politics or race are definitely subjects to avoid discussing during an interview.

Rule 15.
Feedback after selection interviews will help you perform better in future job applications.

Selectors are, in the main, willing to talk to the candidates who did not get the job. They can be a useful source of information about the job market and may suggest strategies that will help you improve your interview technique for the future. It is up to you to make the first approach but polite requests for a debriefing are not usually refused.

Rule 16.
Feedback during appraisal interviews is intended to help you.

Listen to what your manager has to tell you and take advice in the spirit in which it is given. Remember Golden Rule 5: that the purpose of appraisal (and the feedback you are given) is to help you maximise your contribution to the organisation and achieve your personal and professional goals.

Rule 17.
Don't overreact to negative feedback.

None of us are perfect and we all, at times, will face negative feedback on something we have done. If your manager criticises an aspect of your performance it is because he or she feels that there is a problem that needs to be addressed. Be objective; look at the problem rather than feeling an aspect of your personality is being condemned.

Rule 18.
Keep records of your job applications and interviews.

If you are carrying out a systematic job search, you will be making approaches to prospective employers on a regular basis. By keeping clear records of what you have done, you will maintain the momentum of the search and begin to identify aspects of your search that are going particularly well or aspects which are not producing the results you want. Use the same principle to monitor the success of interviews. Take a little time to note what went well and what went badly so that you are well prepared for the next meeting with a selector.

Rule 19.
Keep a record of your daily progress at work.

The interview is only a small part of the appraisal process. Help yourself and your manager to monitor your progress in achieving existing objectives by keeping brief but clear records of your day-to-day work. Use these as the basis for evaluating your own performance and setting future objectives. Where are you performing well? In what areas is there room for improvement?

Rule 20.
Keep working to improve your interview technique.

Confidence in your own abilities will take you a long way towards performing well in an interview, but it is not the only contributory factor. No amount of confidence will help if you cannot communicate clearly with the interviewer. Communication skills, like any other skills, can be developed and improved. It may sometimes seem like hard work but, if you get the result you want, isn't that work worthwhile?

FURTHER READING

There are dozens of books available from high street book stores about interview techniques, particularly for selection interviews. Many titles also give advice on preparing CVs, application forms and letters. You may also find it useful to look at books which give sample tests and prepared answers to interview questions. A word of caution; use these books as guidelines. They offer good advice but *you* are applying for jobs, not the writer. Nobody can take the tests or answer the questions for you!

Useful points of reference for more detailed information include the following books which you will find in libraries or the business section of most book shops:

Fletcher, C. (1993) *Appraisal*, Institute of Personnel Management.

Hodgson, P. & Hodgson, J. (1992) *The Sunday Times Business Skills Series: Effective Meetings*, Century Business.

Holmes, K. (1999) *Job Seeking*, Orion Business.

McIlwee, T. & Roberts, I. (1991) *Human Resource Management*, Elm Publications.

Morris, D. (1994) *Bodytalk: A World Guide to Gestures*, Jonathan Cape.

Shea, M. (1998) *The Primacy Effect*, Orion Business.

Torrington, D. (1994) *International Human Resource Management: Think Globally, Act Locally*, Prentice Hall.

Torrington, D., Weightman, J. & Kirsty, J. (1985) *Management Methods*, Gower.

ACKNOWLEDGEMENTS

Many thanks to all those people who shared their experiences of both selection and appraisal interviews with me during the preparation of this book, and to Helen Woodcock for her perceptive observations. Thanks also to Helicon Publishing for permission to quote from their compilation, *The Hutchinson Dictionary of Business Quotations*.

INDEX